5 Stones For Slaying Giants

"I just read your book, 5 Stones for Slaying Giants, and I was truly blessed. Your book contains practical suggestions for creating success. Everyone should read it!"

Dr. Eli Jones, University Of Houston Excellence In Selling Program

"In a world where so much seems to be hidden by the smoke and mirrors of moral decay, the leaders of American business must once again embrace the ideals which have made this country the world's leading economic power. Curt Tueffert has given us, through the clarity expressed throughout 5 Stones For Slaying Giants, an example-filled methodology for the reaffirmation of fundamental values upon which our free market society has been built. It is a refreshing presentation of value-based judgment and practices that every servant leader can implement day in and day out."

J. Downey Bridgewater, President and Chief Executive Officer
Sterling Bancshares, Inc. and Sterling Bank

"This book is a WINNER! It's written as a story that's loaded with practical tools that can be immediately implemented in your business and in your personal life."

Dr. Tony Alessandra, Author The Platinum Rule and Charisma

"Curt Tueffert's "5 Stones For Slaying Giants" renews and expands my resolve regarding the value of motivational presentations. The message, the unique approach and the genuine passion in delivery create a unique and beneficial experience for anyone fortunate enough to be in the audience."

Louis Garvin, President - Fort Bend Chamber Of Commerce

"Your 5 Stones for Slaying Giants was a huge success among all levels of employees. Not only was everyone energized during the presentation; but it was also the talk of the evening regarding what a learning experience and what a dynamic and energetic speaker you are. Our intent of having a speaker was to offer our employees a great experience, I am confident with your presentation we accomplished that task."

Tim Hekker - CEO/President Hearthstone Assisted Living

"Mr. Tueffert presented 5 Stones For Slaying Giants. He tailored his presentation so that it was relevant to our industry and conveyed a message and lesson the membership could take with them. His presentation was not only entertaining but also enlightening and informative. " I received nothing but positive comments from members and would definitely consider using his services again in the future"

Jennifer Woodruff - Dir. of Marketing & Communications
Houston Builders And Contractors

" Curt has written a powerful and compelling book based on the classic Bible story. His five stones are tools we can all use to slay the giants of negativity, apathy, cynicism and despair. Thus book is both highly inspirational and accessible. It will make a difference in your life- read it today."

Snowden McFall, Author, Fired Up! How to Succeed by Making Your Dreams Come True and 3 other books

"There is a lot of meat in this book. I found myself biting off chunks at a time, going back to various chapters in an effort to absorb the truths and insights discussed and offered. The wisdom found in these pages can be applied to all aspects of life, not just our work lives. Curt's passion for the subject matter literally jumps from the pages"

Quart Graves – Chick-Fil-A Operator

"Even if you pick up only one of Curt's five stones, you will immediately be stated on a path towards a more satisfying and successful career. Curt's unique method of storytelling combined with specific tools makes "5 Stones For Slaying Giants" a must read for anyone who needs inspiration in both their personal and professional lives. It should be required reading for every salesperson and sales manager in our industry."

Sandi Jerome, editor, Digital Dealer magazine

"Buy it! Read it! Live it! Five Stones is essential reading for anyone wanting to excel in life. This exciting book is full of practical ideas that you can immediately use to get better results. Tueffert's system of success is Rock Solid!"

Ruben Gonzalez – Three-time Olympian, Professional Speaker and Trainer

"Curt Tueffert's Five Stones…is provocative and inspiring. His ability to distill the principles of success into five elements is profoundly helpful; and immediately usable by anyone seeking a powerful growth experience."

Don Hutson, CEO U.S. Learning, Inc, Professional Speaker, Author

"WOW…what a powerful book! Pick up one of these five stones and you'll change your life, pick up all five and you'll change the world!"

Rick Butts, Author, Speaker, Marketing Oracle

"Five Stones is a powerful challenge personally. It is even more impacting professionally. Tueffert masterfully applies the strengths of one of the Bible's most commanding personalities to the challenge of modern business culture. The result is a practical guide to success in commerce or any endeavor. I have a son beginning his business career. Five Stones is a must read for him. I will be recommending it for the members of my church more years to come."

Mark S. Hardman – Senior Pastor, Sugar Creek Baptist Church

Curt Tueffert may be contacted for additional information, interviews and speaking engagements by email at tueffert@aol or curt@tueffert.com.

ISBN   1-59196-700-7

Table Of Contents

Introduction

There are many people who have contributed to this book, who need to be recognized. Jim Jacobus (www.teamcer.com) taught me so much about speaking and training and has been instrumental in outlining my thoughts. What I learned about Customer Service was through watching Jim teach and model these principles daily. Many of the ideas and examples that are covered in the 5 Stones came from understanding that Jim and I have similar backgrounds and similar speaking styles. Regarding leadership ability, Quart Graves has modeled Servant Leadership as I worked with him at Digital Consulting. When it comes to sales, Scott Shadle and Larry Collins, who took me under their wing and did not give up, modeled much of my career.

My wife Carla and children (Jake, Kyle, and Aimee) have watched me labor over this work for many hours. As I travel across the US, speaking and training, they have sacrificed many nights with me not at home. My gratitude for their sacrifices goes very deep.

This book is dedicated to the memory of David I. Bloomfield, one of my most valued Knowledge Agents while I was working at Unilearn. I hired David to help launch a new interactive video product to a market that was not quite ready for it. Yes David, I know the "I" in your name is for impatient. Thank you for your spirit and teaching me a few new sales techniques. I miss you.

As you read this book, please keep in mind which of the 5 Stones you currently have and which you want more of in your business, career, and life. Once you understand the impact these stones can have, you'll be slaying giants in no time.

Curt Tueffert
www.tueffert.com
www.slaying-giants.com

Chapter 1 - Slaying Giants, An Example

Then, out from the armies of the Philistines came a champion named Goliath who stood over 9 feet tall...

The sun rose over the valley of Elah on the 40th day of battle. The Israelite army occupied one hill, the Philistine army the other. The valley that separated the two hills served another purpose; it was the place where the two great armies met twice daily and drew their battle lines.

King Saul led the Israelite army. Saul was a seasoned battle hero who led his troops into many previous victories. The Israelites were a special group of people destined for greatness and hand picked by God. Their mission was to rid the land of these Philistines. Saul entered this battle 39 days ago, confident and committed to the mission. That was 39 long days in the past. "Would this be our day of victory?" Saul pondered, "Who among us will answer the challenge of these Philistines?"

On the opposite hill where the Philistine army camped the mood was different. There was energy and excitement in the air. For 39 days the Philistine army gathered in the valley to face the dreaded Israelites. Daily, the Philistines grew more confident when their challenge for battle was met with fear and no opposition. The Philistine army knew Saul was afraid of their champion.

Goliath of Gath was the hero and defender of the Philistine army. Goliath was career military. From his youth he dreamed of being a great warrior, one that legends would be written of. From his earliest age he trained to be a great warrior and soldier serving his commander. Goliath had a few advantages that made him a fierce contender. He stood over nine feet tall. Some estimate that he stood 9' 6". His armor weighed 125 pounds, while the head of his spear weighed close to 15 pounds. He was fit, strong, and well versed in the art of war. Twice a day for the past 39 days Goliath would gather his troops in the Valley of Elah, and state this challenge to the Israelites:

"Choose a man among you to fight me, if you have one. If he is able to fight and kill me, we will be your slaves. But if I overtake him and kill him, you and King Saul will be our slaves."

In the camp of the Israelites Saul was losing his confidence and the morale of his troops was low. Twice daily he'd tried his best motivational speeches. He reminded his men of past victories. He reminded his men of their rich heritage. They were the army of the living God, right? Saul added a bonus of his daughter in marriage and tax favor to anyone who took Goliath on and won. The men heard only the challenge of Goliath. And now, Goliath was ridiculing the Israelite army. He poked fun of their God, their king, and their women. The taunting was relentless. Still, not one person rose to Goliath's challenge.

On the 40th day of battle, the sun rose in the Bethlehem valley where a small boy named David who was serving his father by tending a flock of sheep. Early that morning, a messenger came to David and told him to go back home, his father needed him. When David returned home, his father Jesse asked him to go to the battlefield and deliver some bread to David's three older brothers and some cheese to the commander. The delivery of food was to check on his sons and to insure favor from the commander.

David arrived just in time. The army of God was gathering to put their battle weapons together, shouting the battle cry, and lining up in the valley for this day's verbal challenge. "This is exciting", David thought. Goliath came out and gave his daily challenge and added a heavy dose of sarcasm. This made the army of Israel run away from him with great fear. The soldiers explained to David the challenge and the bounty that King Saul promised to the man who would fight. The king's daughter in marriage and tax exemption for him and their extended family was the hero's prize.

David could barely contain his anger. "Who is this uncircumcised Philistine that he should defy the armies of the living God?" replied David. The soldiers repeated to him what the prize would be if someone fought Goliath and won. Word got back to Saul that a young boy was in the camp, asking about this Goliath soldier and the outcome of his defeat. Quickly David found himself before Saul explaining that he would like to challenge Goliath. "You are only a boy David, and Goliath has been a fighting warrior all his life. It would not be a fair fight," said Saul. David stood and defended his position. He told King Saul of the sheep his father trusted to him. Once, a bear came into his camp and seized one of his prized sheep. He wrestled the bear to the ground and killed him. Another time, a lion entered the camp, and took an animal in his mouth. David killed that lion without hurting the sheep. David said, "The Lord who delivered me from the paw of the lion and the paw of the bear will deliver me from the hand of this Philistine."

Saul was in no position to argue. Morale was low and he was losing the last of his own confidence. Could he entrust the destiny of his soldiers to a boy no older than fourteen? This was a difficult decision for Saul to make. "Where were all the other warriors?" Saul thought. "Was there no other soldier in the camp willing to fight Goliath?" As Saul considered how David had spoken with such passion and confidence, Saul's hope was restored. David's battle with a lion and a bear was no match for Goliath, yet there was something in the character of David that Saul respected. He was regaining a vision of victory for this Philistine battle and the restoration of confidence in his men.

Saul suited David in his personal armor, a special cut made for the king. David looked silly in Saul's armor dressed for battle. He tried to walk around the tent. His steps were awkward and this armor was very heavy. The armor prevented movement for the small boy. He removed Saul's armor and settled for something simple, his own clothes and his sling.

Grabbing his staff, David walked down to a small brook. Bending down, he gathered five smooth stones. These were stones for slaying giants. "Let me see," thought David, "one stone for Goliath, and one for each of his brothers, just in case they get angry when I kill their brother." David placed these five stones for slaying giants in his pouch and entered the battlefield.

Meanwhile, Goliath heard that the Israelites had finally found a soldier, a brave warrior to fight him. "It's about time," thought Goliath. "This will be over quickly." When Goliath first saw this small boy standing his ground on the battlefield, he thought it was a joke. "Am I a dog, that you come at me with sticks?" shouted Goliath. Then Goliath began to really curse the Israelite army, King Saul, David, and the God they served. Goliath began to burn with anger and rage. "They sent this boy out here to mock me," thought Goliath.

As Goliath settled down, David spoke up. "You come against me with sword and spear. You mock my people, my king, and my God. I come against you in the name of my God, the Lord Almighty. Today, He will hand you over to me. Today, I will strike you down and cut off your head. Today, I will feed your dead body and the bodies of all your soldiers to the animals. Today, the whole world will know that there is a God in Israel. Goliath, prepare to die!"

Goliath shouted a battle cry that could be heard across both camps. He began to charge David, ready to grab him by the hands and tear him in two. David moved quicker. Reaching into his pouch, he grabbed one of his smooth stones, just right for slaying giants, and placed it in his sling. With one fluid motion of running and placing the stone in the sling, David whipped it around twice and launched the stone. David's stone found the mark, the center of Goliath's massive forehead. The stone sank deep into his forehead and Goliath fell facedown into the dirt. David did not stop there, still running toward Goliath, he grabbed the sword of this dead Philistine and cut off his head.

Silence surrounded both camps. It was the silence of amazement. The silence of true disbelief. Then the reality set in. Saul's army, the army of the living God, had won. Against all odds, a young boy rose to the challenge and won. Saul knew the battle had just turned around. No longer was the Israelite army weak and cowardly. No longer were they afraid to fight. Victory was in front of them as David, a boy of 12, defeated Goliath at his own game.

Across the Philistine camp, another reality set in. They had lost. Against all odds, some kid had bested their hero, their champion, and their master warrior. And it was not over. What they saw in the eyes of their enemy was a renewed confidence, a passion burning inside, a vision of extended victory, and the value of exterminating the rest of the Philistine army. It took a split second for them to feel the impact. They turned and ran; yet it was too late. They met their death in the Valley of Elah.

When David stopped at the stream to pick up his five stones, he selected weapons you can use to slay the giants in your life. The five stones represent Passion, Excellence, Vision, Value, and Confidence. With these, you can defeat the giants that create battles in your professional and personal life. With these stones you can win.

Chapter 2 - Stone #1 – Passion

"Whatever your life's work is, do it well. A man should do his job so well that the living, the dead, and the unborn could do it no better"
Martin Luther King

For David to have faced Goliath, he needed passion. Passion can imply a strong emotion that has an overpowering or compelling effect. When David saw the faces of the troops and heard the taunting of Goliath, his passion began to burn. Something inside him answered the call. Call it passion, fervor, ardor, enthusiasm, or zeal, I think David had each of these burning hot; so hot that he answered the call to fight Goliath without hesitation or doubt.

What makes winners win? Regardless of what they are winning, something fuels them. I've seen this in athletes, business leaders, sales professionals, teachers, and ministers. One of the winning ingredients fueling them is passion. Mother Teresa was passionate for the poor and helpless. She spent her whole life helping others. Jack Welch, the former head of General Electric was passionate about his people and GE's impact on worldwide business. He grew GE into a powerhouse that has impacted our global economy. Phil Jackson is passionate about coaching winning basketball teams like the Chicago Bulls and the Los Angeles Lakers. Phil has taken both teams to heights previously unseen. For you and I to slay the giants in our lives, we need that emotion which drives us, which pushes us forward, demanding our energy and our attention. We need passion!

After speaking to a large group of professionals on this subject, a woman came up to me and asked a simple question," Where do I get this passion?" That question drew me back to an event, which ignited my passion for my profession.

While attending college, I was the youth pastor for a small church in Southern California. After one Sunday service, our senior pastor gave me a flyer about an event to be held in a few months. The event called "College Briefing" would be held in August at Forest Home, a camp tucked in the hills of Southern California. The legacy of Forest Home is rich and deep. Passionate Christian leaders such as Billy Graham and Bill Bright (Campus Crusade For Christ) have had their passion ignited at Forest Home. The idea behind College Briefing was to prepare students for college by exposing them to strong Biblical teaching and encouragement. I was already interested from what I had seen and heard of this event. Then my eyes fell on the name of the guest speaker; Dr. Tony Campolo! I'd been listening to one of his tapes and really wanted the chance to meet him and hear him in person.

Since our youth group was very small, the church agreed to send my wife and me to attend College Briefing as leaders, sharing a cabin with the college students and leading the small group discussions after Dr. Campolo finished the main sessions. During one of these his lectures, Tony Campolo said,

"Human Existence is just the meaningless passage of time, between all too few moments of genuine aliveness."

I heard it, wrote it down, and read it again. He said it twice. I knew, at that moment, I would become passionate about the things that fueled me. Campolo continued driving his point home that the world is full of "dead" people. People, who claim to be alive, but are really dead on the inside. The lights are on, yet nobody is home! These people lead quiet lives of desperation, never really living to their full potential, and yet, not really dead, they just merely exist. He challenged us to lead lives of genuine aliveness, fully engaged in the essence of life. To engage with people is to transfer energy and passion between each other, and not continue to suck the life out of each other. As we debriefed these sessions with the college students, I could see they were impacted as well. I could see how they related to what was said and wanted to become more alive to what really mattered. When I returned to my job, after College Briefing, I saw Dr. Campolo's analogy at work, where employees where physically present and far away mentally. Later, I also saw this at the University, with professors who lost their passion for teaching, yet continued teaching based on status and duty. I knew I would never be the same.

The woman who stopped me after that meeting continued to listen. As I explained this lengthy answer to her question "Where do I get this passion?" she now understood after hearing my story. She realized that passion had to come from and burn inside, not just glow. It must grow strong enough to be compelling and overpowering. It must to drive you forward, to action.

Passion has a way of reducing or removing fear of failure. When Goliath fired up his troops by ridiculing the Israelite army, it made David even more resolved to fight and win. Let's face it; if you were 12 years old and asked to fight a 9-foot giant, who has trained all his life in the art of combat, would you take the challenge? You, a logical thinker, would quickly determine that the odds are stacked against you. Fear of failure and certain death would overtake your thought and action process! King Saul offered David some armor as protection. David quickly determined this was not going to work and stayed with his original plan. David was fearless in his zeal to slay Goliath. Are you fearless in slaying the giants that block your path?

Passion has a way of building confidence (see stone #5). Coaches draw upon the player's passion before the big football game. The locker room speech is designed to fire up the team, to ignite zeal, enthusiasm, and fervor for the pending victory. Passion is what Michael Jordan had when he'd practice shooting free throws two hours before each basketball game. Passion is what fuels golf legend Tiger Woods to work on his game after the tournament is over. Tiger Woods will continue to practice his putting long after the crowds have left. He is driven to perfection and it shows in his game. Passion drives the business owner to come early and stay late. It sparks the entrepreneur to risk everything on a new business idea. Passion fuels the leader to invest in his people and his team. Passion drives the sales professional to ask a few more questions, probe a little deeper, and seek more understanding before offering a solution. Selling is a profession where rejection is frequent, yet passion continues to move you forward, past the rejection and onto the next sale. Passion is what causes parents to sacrifice their personal needs and desires for the needs of their children.

How can passion slay the giants in your life? Arnold Glasow said it best,

"Nothing splendid was ever created in cold blood. Heat is required to forge anything. Every great accomplishment is the story of a flaming heart."

When discussing passion, you need to determine if you have it at all. Gordon MacDonald in his book, *Restoring Your Spiritual Passion*, concludes that restoration contains three critical elements; Safe Places, Still Times, and Special Friends.

Safe Places

Safe places allow you to lower your defenses and relax. This clears the mind of anxious thoughts, giving room for clear thinking. Finding a place to get away can flame the heart with the required heat to forge your passion. A safe place is also free of defense mechanisms that prevent you from relaxing. One of my safe places is at the beach, watching the waves rolling in. This calming scene allows me to take a deep breath and get ready to ignite the passions in my life. While living in San Diego, California, I was transferred to Portland, Oregon. I knew this would be a stressful transition for my family. Leaving friends and family and starting with a new company would cause unwanted stress for everyone. I went to the beach to gather my thoughts and prepare for this new chapter in my career. There would be stress and new demands, yet I knew why I was taking the transfer and how my family would benefit from this. I used this safe place to gain the passion required to make the transition from San Diego to Portland. It really helped as we arrived in Portland. The first major change was the weather. San Diego is famous for perfect weather, lots of sunshine, coastal breezes and romantic beaches. Portland is known for having 7-9 months of rain with occasional interruptions of sunshine. That was a major challenge for us. Yet, we reveled in the times when the sun was shining and really enjoyed the Pacific Northwest by hiking and exploring all the wonders of this glorious and beautiful mountainous location.

Still Times

Still times are blocks of time where clear thinking can create or ignite passions that have been suppressed. 'Still times' allow reflection of goals and desires, creation of plans, hopes, and dreams. When you feel safe and still, you can build on the reflection and creation of your dreams and plans. During these still times, bring something to write on. I recommend a blank notebook or journal. Use the empty pages as an opportunity to fill them with your clear thinking. Write a list of what you need to make things happen in different area of your life. Make sure you write as much as you can, so you can capture all your ideas and thoughts. Pour out your ideas and creative dreams so that you can assemble them later into the prioritized list for impact and purpose. When I started Brick Wall Motivation, I had many ideas and goals for this new company. My thoughts raced so quickly, I felt like I was jumping from one thought to another with no logical direction. As I wrote my thoughts and ideas down, I began to see the bigger picture and design for Brick Wall Motivation. I saw what was required then and what could be postponed for a few months, perhaps a few years. I wrote down what I wanted Brick Wall Motivation to represent for my clients and me. I began to fill the empty pages of my journal with the ideas for the foundation of my new company. Still times give you clarity and focus. Treasure them.

Special Friends

Special friends are there to encourage you and hold you accountable. It's easy to find people that wish you well. It is difficult to find special friends who will hold you accountable on your journey to slay the giants. There are people in your life that wish you success and those who wish you failure. Make sure you align yourself with the right ones, those who build you up. Special friends know you and know your motives. They offer a listening ear, advice, counsel, and sometimes a shoulder to lean on. By nature, I tend to take on too many commitments. This frustrates the people in my life that are counting on me to fulfill these commitments. During my Youth Ministry days, I was a leader in Young Life, a great ministry to high school students. Taking on this ministry, a full college schedule, and a part-time job, I was in my element of over-commitment. A group of leaders from our Young Life staff came and helped me work out all my priorities and helped me determine the cause of this need to over-commit. They where very special friends who took their own time to help me make time. In fact, with their advice and counsel, I decided to leave the Young Life ministry to focus on my college work. That was a tough decision, and could only be made with the help of friends who cared to enough to help me focus my passion.

Once you have safe places, still times, and special friends, get to the task. As Robert Schuller put it, "I'd rather attempt to do something great and fail than to attempt to do nothing and succeed." You must create action. David accepted the challenge from Goliath and fought. He did not hang around the soldiers asking their opinion. He just did it.

"Flaming enthusiasm, backed up by horse sense and persistence, is the quality that most frequently makes for success." – Dale Carnegie

A few years ago, I worked with a group of sales professionals in the software industry. At the end of a two-day sales training class, I gave them a challenge. Each attendee was to take two new ideas and begin to integrate them into their daily lives. Some of the sales professionals even committed to try these new ideas the next business day. They were passionate about these new ideas and felt sure they would help them close more business. I checked back with the group 3 months later to review the progress and to answer additional questions. Each one returned to their old habits, expecting different results. They failed to take their passion to the next level. They took no action. Passion requires action. You must take action.

Putting Stone #1 (Passion) Into Action

- When you think of passion, what comes to mind? Write down some of your thoughts and experiences with passion.

- What is your fear of failure? How can passion reduce or remove the fear?

- Write down all the passionate people in your life who have influenced you. How have they influenced you?

- Where are your safe places? When was the last time you retreated there? What could you do at your safe place to restore your passion?

- Still Times? Invest in a journal and begin writing down your passionate thoughts, your dreams, hopes, goals, and desires. What will it take for you to move toward them?

- Who are your special friends that can help you slay your giants? How can they help you slay your giants?

- What three things can you do today to place your passion into action? Who will be impacted?

Chapter 3 - Stone #2 – Excellence

"The quality of a person's life is in direct proportion to their commitment to excellence, regardless of their chosen field of endeavor." Vince Lombardi

How can a 12-year-old boy, armed with his sling and a stone, defeat a seasoned warrior on the first try? I've been reading the David and Goliath story since my youth and always pondered that fact. My conclusion, David demanded excellence in all that he did, even as a boy. Killing both a bear and a lion that attacked his flock already proved his excellence with a knife. Now, his prowess with a sling was used to stop the taunting of the opposing army. It comes down to excellence. For you to succeed in slaying the giants in your life, you must commit to excellence. Excellence is being the best you can be, being #1, winning the prize, or however you define it.

I love reading Stephen Covey's work, so let's begin with the end in mind. To begin with the end in mind says Covey, is to start with a clear understanding of your destination. It means to know where you're going so that you better understand where you are now and so that the steps you take are always in the right direction. (*7 Habits Of Highly Effective People*). When you have a goal in mind and you know where you are now, then you can determine the right steps to get you to your goal. Covey also stated that this is based on the principle that all things are created twice. The first is a mental creation, and the second physical.

Applying this to your commitment to excellence, you need a clear picture of what the end result will be and how you plan to get there. Once you see it in your "mind's eye" (first creation), then you can then create the action steps (physical creation) to make it happen.

In June of 1999, I picked up the mail and saw an interesting invitation to spend 5 days on the beautiful beaches of Cozamel in the Gulf of Mexico. The post card had a date and hotel location for an initial meeting where the details would be provided. I was interested, so I went. When I arrived at the hotel, I was welcomed by a group of people wearing Team In Training™ shirts, sponsored by the Leukemia Society of America. The idea was to sign up to run a marathon, plus do the required fundraising to earn your "free trip" to Cozamel and run the 26.2 miles! What was I thinking running a marathon?

It was June and the marathon was scheduled for November, five months away. Could I really train and get in shape to run a marathon, plus raise the required funding amount in only five short months? The Goliath that taunted me said "You, a runner? You'll quit before summer is over. Loser!" I needed the right picture of the end result. Once I had that, I had the first creation completed, and the second creation started. The Leukemia Society's Team In Training members held many meetings to help. They gave me the training schedule and provided group runs to get in shape for the marathon. They also matched each runner with a child sponsor, stricken with this deadly cancer. Matthew was my little guy. Matthew was 5 years old and full of life. At the time, his cancer was in remission. I made it a point to meet Matthew and his parents. I wanted to have his picture and his life in my mind each time I trained. In doing this, I trained and ran for Matthew. Summer training in Houston, Texas is not easy. The heat and humidity can beat you down. Yet, I had a clear picture of Matthew and of me crossing the finish line in Cozumel, Mexico only a few months later. I was committed to excellence in my training and in all other areas that would impact my training. There was numerous times where I began to doubt, where I began to argue in my mind the whole purpose of this adventure. It would have been easy not to strive for excellence and to cut corners in my training and my diet. What was I thinking? So I kept going back to Safe Places, Still Times and Special Friends to keep my passion level high. During the training, we were assigned a coach who trained with us every Saturday morning. Our team arrived at 5:15am to run as a group. Coach Chris would run with us, to increase our skill and endurance. He taught us how to pace, how to identify potential areas of pain, and how to train individually during the week. Coach Chris was also at the marathon, running short distances with each one on his team, cheering and motivating us toward the finish line. As I cross the finish line, completing 26.2 miles, I faced my giant for the last time. I heard his taunting, yet it was too late, I'd already crossed the finish line. With a fresh stone in my sling, I let it fly. He never had a chance! Without passion, excellence, and the goal in mind, I would have settled for something far less. Perhaps I would have talked myself out of the race altogether. I attribute my determination to complete the marathon on my passion to win and my desire to train with excellence.

Another element of excellence is research. People committed to excellence take the time to research, study and learn from those who've already been successful in their chosen field. They seek to understand the skills and resources required before starting in that field. People who strive for business excellence study other business leaders who have made it. They become students of learning and research. They want to know how to keep the end in mind. They do research as a goal, a purpose, and an outcome. They do research with laser like focus so that they can prevent some of the mistakes others have made.

Scott Shadle strives for excellence by doing research. When I first met Scott, he was the National Sales Manager for a small computer distributor in San Diego, California. Scott wanted to hire a sales person to help expand the company's distribution network. I thought of him as someone who was always thinking of ways to learn more. Scott hired me to join his team as a sales professional. When I took the sales position, I reported to Scott. I always looked forward to Mondays. It never failed that Scott would come to work Monday morning with great new ideas to sell more product. When I asked about the source of these ideas, he told me about all the books he was reading, the trade papers he scanned, and other sources for good information. He constantly researched the trends and movements in our industry to seek out a competitive advantage. That was almost 20 years ago and he still strives for excellence by researching and learning about his industry.

When it came to understanding sales and the hands on sales training, Scott taught me to ask questions based on the research I'd previously done. By asking strong open questions and by seeking to gain answers, I would gain more data, more of a foundation to build a favorable conclusion. I watched him do this in many sales meetings, business negotiations, and other events where his probing for information became the basis for his solutions in various business settings. There is an art to asking good questions. These questions do not just appear in your mind. Good questions are prepared in advance. Doctors, lawyers, attorneys, accountants, counselors and sales people all ask strong, probing questions to get to the heart of the matter. The difference between a good questions and great questions is in the response. Did the response require deep thought, reflection, and perhaps some research? If so, the question asked was very good. Was it asked at the right time, with the right supporting data? If so, then the one asking the question spent time preparing for event. Scott taught me that and a whole lot more. He taught me the value of research and preparation before the sales call.

Excellence is a critical stone for slaying giants. If you are fighting a battle in your career, do the research. If you are in combat in your relationships, read and seek out strong sources of knowledge. If you are in sales and you feel you're in a slump, read a good sales book, and heed the time-honored words of Zig Ziglar, Jim Rohn or Tom Hopkins. If you are in a position of leadership, study the books from John C. Maxwell, an authority on leadership principles and issues. If you cannot see yourself as a success then start researching those who've made it and are willing to give you the tools, skills, and vision to do the same.

A great example of those who have made it can be found in three specific areas; business, sports, and academics. Tim Wackel, president of The Wackel Group (www.thewackelgroup.com) is a professional sales trainer who spent 16 years in one of America's top computer manufactures. Tim's excellence came in the form of presentation practice. Tim rehearses and outlines each of his presentations to a level of excellence I have not seen. I had the privilege of working with Tim in the summer of 2002. We were rolling out a WOW! Customer Service course for 1100 employees of a casino. Tim, at 5:00am, was rehearing and timing his 8-hour presentation in his hotel room to the company of just pillows, towels, and empty chairs in his hotel room.

Regarding sports, two people come to mind; Mike Lambresi and Ed Currie. Mike was a 3 time national surfer from California. Mike and I lived in the same development and as I would go to work each early morning, Mike would be heading for any number of local surf spots. What made him excellent was his discipline and demand for excellence in his training. It did not matter if there was no surf or large waves, Mike was always out there, putting in 3 – 6 hours a day, training, practicing, and striving for excellence. Ed Currie had the same passion and demand for excellence in Water Polo. Ed and I attended the same high school and we quickly discovered Ed's natural talent for this sport. His practice and demand for excellence landed him at Occidental College where he was the captain of the Water Polo team, competed for regional and statewide titles and continue to play competitively long after college, where he toured in Australia on a men's team.

When it comes to academic excellence, Dr. Eli Jones (www.elijones.com) has impacted the world of sales like no other person. Dr. Jones gave up a 15-year career in sales to help develop the Excellence In Selling program at the University of Houston. This program is currently the largest program in any college or university in the US and has earned respect from business leaders for the caliber of professional sales person this program graduates. Dr. Jones continues to develop the program by developing new professors, enhancing the curriculum, and promoting the program throughout the Houston area. In addition, he strives for excellence by publishing various articles and research findings in top academic and business publications. What causes these people to be at the top of their game in business, sports, and academic circles? The answer is passion for their chosen gift and the internal demand for excellence. Without these professionals constantly pushing the level of excellence, where would that level settle?

The last element of excellence is networking. Great leaders have built a network of people around them. Great parents have support groups in their churches, neighborhoods, and extended families. Great athletes train with other great athletes to push them harder, keeping their commitment of excellence in their game. They network with other great athletes constantly influencing and being influenced.

"Networking creates a power that leads to a richer, fuller personal and professional life," says Donna Fisher and Sandy Vilas in *Power Networking* (*55 Secrets for Personal and Professional Success*). Networking brings you in contact with people who know people. Fisher and Vilas state:

"A referral generates 80% more results than a cold call. Approximately 70% of all jobs are found through networking. Most people you meet have at least 250 contacts. Anyone you might want to meet or contact is only four or five people away from you." (*Power Networking*)

How does that apply to you? Let's say you have committed to excellence in your professional career and you would like to meet other business executives that run large corporations. The purpose of networking is to meet other people that can help you strive for excellence and reach your goal. By networking, you can ask your immediate circle of influence who they know that knows someone who runs a large corporation. There is a high probability a match is close by. Once you begin to network, take an active interest in that person's business and the role they play to influence the business. Ask them how you can help them and their business goals. Taking an active interest can begin by asking great questions based on the research you have done. In my experience, the better the question, the more the other person wants to talk. Successful networkers are more interested in other people and show their interest by the questions they ask. I belong to a local chapter of Business Network International (BNI) where we meet weekly to network and exchange leads. I see some business people coming to a meeting or an event to "pump" others for information so they can be self-promoting. That does not work well in professional networking. I've seen others take an active interest, seeking to understand the other person by asking good questions. They tend to get leads and to be remembered long after the networking event has passed.

When I first started speaking professionally, I wanted to meet other speakers who where successful. I had a business contact that knew Jack Canfield, who co-wrote many of *the Chicken Soup For The Soul* books with Mark Victor Hansen. Through this contact, it was arranged that I would call Jack Canfield at his home. I was in a phone booth on a busy street corner when I called Mr. Canfield. He gave me 15 minutes and I asked him many questions regarding the profession of speaking, his opinion on that future direction of the business and some advice for people like me. What Mr. Canfield said confirmed what I've heard from other speakers. To break into this business, speak everywhere you can, to anyone that will listen, on topics you are passionate about. I began to build a network of contacts in the speaking world, where I could ask questions and gain further insight. This really helped to move my speaking career forward as I listened and took notes on what these experts said and did to promote their careers.

Brian Tracy best summarized the quest for excellence when he said,

"All successful men and women are big dreamers. They imagine what their future could be, ideal in every respect, and then they work every day toward their distant vision, that goal or purpose."

It starts with the end in mind. Then you develop the mental creation, next the physical creation (the action steps). Then you work towards it, every day! When you commit to excellence you must strive for it every day. David struck Goliath directly on the forehead because he worked and practiced with his sling ability, every day. He needed that skill to protect his sheep from harm. He did not commit to excellence specifically to fight in the battle with Goliath. Yet, when the time came, his practice paid off.

One of the greatest football coaches of all time was Tom Landry. Landry's ability to coach and his commitment to excellence were legendary. It is said that he created a Dallas Cowboy's philosophy. Modified and enhanced by some on his staff, a sign still hangs in the Cowboy's locker room:

The value of a man's life is in direct proportion to his commitment to excellence.

Where is your commitment to excellence? Pick a handful of areas in your life where you are committed. Now reduce that list to between three and five. Prioritize your list based on importance and start the process. The outcome will be in direct proportion to the amount of energy you spend going for your prize or goal.

Putting Stone #2 (Excellence) Into Action

- What plans and purpose do you have where you have a mental picture of what you want? How are you going to achieve your vision?

- How committed are you to excellence? What will it take to get there? What steps are in place to move you forward?

- What research and study have you done lately that builds your passion and commitment for excellence?

- What is the size and strength of your network? How are you giving back to your network to make it stronger?

- What are you doing to expand your network? Remember, it not about all the people you know, it is about all the people who know you!

Chapter 4 - Stone #3 – Vision

"Where there is no vision, the people perish" (Proverbs 29:18 KJV)

David, still a boy, was wise beyond his youth. I believe David realized the immediate need of King Saul and his army. He saw the dejection, the shame, and the doubt on the faces of each soldier. David heard the complaining and the grumbling inside the ranks of men. "Will anyone take this Goliath? How they will treat us when we are captured?" David also saw beyond that moment and the victory he was prepared to participate in. People with vision see possibilities where others only see impossibilities. People with vision are future thinkers. David said it best, "Who is this uncircumcised Philistine that he should taunt the armies of the living God?" (1 Samuel 17:26) David knew the outcome before it started, in his mind's eye he saw Goliath dead on the ground.

Charles Garfield, in his research and study of peak performers worked with business people, leaders, and athletes. His goal was to unlock the secrets of peak performers. Garfield discovered that peak performers are visionary. They strive to see it, feel it, and experience it before it happens. *Peak Performers – The New Heroes of American Business* is Garfield's book outlining what he discovered while researching top performers.

In my research and discussions with leaders and top performers, I have discovered that without a clear vision, the people [employees, culture, energy] do perish. By perish I mean that business failures happen more frequently, employees tend to turnover quicker, and a lack of motivation and morale problems creep in. There are two types of vision that will help you slay your giants; Personal Vision and Corporate Vision.

A personal vision is one where you see yourself achieving the goal. Working with sales people, I ask them what their personal goals are. Why are they in sales?

What challenges keep them from success? Where do they see themselves going and growing? When they can articulate their vision of the future, I can link their selling skills and performance directly to their vision. I can provide peak performers the resources they need to achieve their vision. For those who are challenged with defining their vision, the planning process is critical to their long-term success.

A vision that is personal creates a great sense of ownership and responsibility. Someone serious about growing their business or reaching their sales goals will commit to doing the market research, investing in marketing promotions, and perfecting their sales techniques to reach their sales goals. Business owners and managers of sales teams, regularly create a forecast of sales. Business planning, financial reporting, and creating incentives for sales people will move you toward your vision of where your company can go once you set the goals in place and commit to all the action steps to get there.

An employee that has a personal vision to grow in their career will study and work hard to learn new skills to advance. They will meet the right people, ask the right questions, and position themselves with hard work to earn their advancements. Through their hard work, more challenging responsibilities will present themselves. More people will see their work and the increased value of that work. If their goal is advancement and responsibility, it will come from their personal vision to grow and expand their horizons. Jim Jacobus, the owner of Champion Education Resources (www.teamcer.com) talks about ways to get to WOW! One way is to *act like an owner*". He draws the parallel that owners come in early and stay late when it's their company. When it is your vision and goals, you need to come in early and stay late, making sure you take the responsibility for your personal and professional achievements.

A corporate vision creates a commitment of excellence within business cultures, work teams, and other groups of people who share a common goal. The corporate vision is tied affects others (team, staff, company, client, etc.) Examples of strong corporate vision are Southwest Airlines, UPS (United Parcel Service) and Seattle's Pike Place Fish Market. Southwest Airlines has remained profitable when many of the larger airlines are scrambling for cash. They delight their customers and make it fun to fly simply by giving a smile, having a sense of play, and focusing on the needs of the passenger. UPS approaches a corporate vision with efficiency. Each step in the process of picking up and delivering packages is met with methodical care and planning. Their vision is to be the most efficient shipping company by reducing the number of steps in the shipping process and by standardizing each process to a repeatable and predictable outcome. Pike Place Fish Market's vision has been captured in the phenomenal international bestseller *FISH*! The vision of Pike Place is based on four principles; Choose Your Attitude, Play, Be There, and Make Their Day. These have been captured in *FISH* where thousands of businesses have adopted these four principles in their vision statements and in the hearts and minds of their employees.

Mission statements are created to solidify the team and give them a vision for keeping the end in mind.   Garfield, in his work with peak performers discovered that these people who are striving for excellence all have a basic drive:

"To stand out, to excel in achieving something uniquely one's own that one cares about deeply, and simultaneously to stand in, to excel in achieving something important to others (one's organization, team or family). These are the dual needs of autonomy and affiliation, the twin aspects of mission statements. With them a peak performer lives a dual life, wanting both the rewards of uniqueness and the pride of belonging (to a good family, a winning team, a strong country, a successful planet)." Peak Performers pg. 79.

This basic drive can be placed in tightly worded corporate mission statement that communicates vision. Each employee can then stand out (independent vision) and stand in (the vision to be part of a winning team). Examples of corporate vision, communicated in their mission statements include the Ritz-Carlson Credo:

The Credo

The Ritz-Carlton Hotel is a
place where the genuine care
and comfort of our guests is
our highest mission.

We pledge to provide the finest
personal service and facilities
for our guests who will always
enjoy a warm, relaxed, yet
refined ambience.

The Ritz-Carlton experience
enlivens the senses, instills
well-being, and fulfills even
the unexpressed wishes
and needs of our guests.

The Credo shows the placement of value directly on the guests. Since the mission of Ritz-Carlton is the care and comfort of their guests, all employees go to great lengths to complete this mission. In turn, guests receive the finest service possible. If you have ever stayed at one of their locations, you'll quickly realize that everything they stand for surrounds you from the moment you enter to the moment you leave.

Digital Consulting and Software Services, (www.dcss.com), a Texas based high-end consulting company has a similar vision for both their employees and their clients. They strive to live their mission statement in every way.

"While focusing on the needs of clients, employees, and partners, DCSS strives to be a cost-effective provider of quality information solutions where integrity comes first, and everyone benefits". (DCSS Mission Statement)

DCSS firmly believes that the reputation of the company is lived in the lives of the consultants and employees that serve the customer. To that end, they passionately demand that each employee commit to memorizing both the mission statement and the company philosophy. By living the mission statement both at work and in their personal lives, the employees and consultants who work for DCSS are a different breed. Many clients and partners can tell story after story of heroic deeds done by the DCSS staff on behalf of the client. From last minute rush deliveries to protecting valuable equipment in jeopardy of being destroyed in a rainstorm, these employees live their mission statement. They have vision, a vision for what can be done to improve the reputation, value, and integrity of the company by giving outstanding service to their clients.

The last element of corporate vision is how the actions will impact other people such as a team or staff. We have heard about countless examples of coaches who have drilled plays and scenarios into the minds and bodies of their team. Over and over again they go through the drills and the formations. Why? The coach demands that these drills become rote in the minds of the players so that they can be executed flawlessly without thinking. The corporate vision of the coach is for his team to win at the end of the season. So the actions taken during the season should add up to the final event, the chance to win their division, state, or national title.

How did David's vision impact the Israelite soldiers and King Saul? By the time David came on the scene, Saul was losing his vision, his leadership and his confidence. The men were grumbling and some perhaps were turning on their king with negative talk or other thoughts of defection. David's vision was for the immediate slaying of Goliath and yet, a much deeper impact came. David knew he represented the army of the living God, a vision of greatness, of power and predestined confidence. No 9-foot giant was going to take that away from him. His action gave Saul's army the confidence and courage to charge against the Philistines and to pursue them to the death. It took the vision of one small boy to impact an entire army of seasoned soldiers.

While training for the Cozamel marathon, I was striving for excellence while keeping a specific vision in front of me. I trained by myself and with my local team for one specific purpose, to beat Leukemia by our efforts to raise support and run this marathon. I combined both a Personal and Corporate Vision to help me get out of a warm bed to face a cold run. When I felt like I could not take another step, I saw the face of my sponsor child, and I visualized him at the sidelines cheering me on. To really get me going, I visualized him during a Chemotherapy treatment, getting hit with radiation doses. Then I asked myself, do I really have an excuse not to train? Without these visions, my training would have perished.

Putting Stone #3 (Vision) Into Action

- What is your vision? Have you communicated that to anyone? Take some time and write out the vision you have for your business, your career, your family, and yourself. Be crystal clear in your thoughts and in your words. What does it sound like, feel like, smell like and taste like? Can you see it in your mind's eye?

- With your vision(s) written down, what will it take to get there? What are the costs you need to count in order to achieve your vision? Write them down.

- Often, we can associate pictures with our goals and vision. Can you find a photograph or a clipping from a magazine that represents your vision? How does that make it easier to see?

- Now, take your vision to another trusted person. Share it with them and ask them to hold you accountable for the outcome and the success. Listen to their comments and their instruction. Be open to comments and suggestions to complete your vision.

Chapter 5 - Stone #4 – Value

"You are not here merely to make a living. You are here in order to enable the world to live more amply, with greater vision, with a finer spirit of hope and achievement. You are here to enrich the world, and you impoverish yourself if you forget the errand." Woodrow Wilson

As David prepared to fight Goliath, his passion, commitment to excellence, and vision would help to add the value he provided to King Saul and his army. He knew the outcome of this battle belonged to his king. He was about to turn the battle around, placing a high value on himself, his father, his brothers, and his fellow soldiers. The value he gave added so much more to the equation.

What is value? How do you determine the value of a person and their actions? To think highly of, to esteem, and to ascribe worth are all part of the definition of value.

Albert Einstein said, *"Try not to be a man of success, rather, a man of value."* Those words have stayed with me throughout my career. In my twenties, I struggled with my ability to add value. As a new sales rep for a computer distributor, I was focused on promoting the different products we sold simply by knowing what they did and how much they cost. My primary concern was being heard and promoting my company. It never occurred to me that I was selling to Value Added Resellers, small business owners who added value by providing a level of service bundled around the products I sold.

Shortly after I started, Larry Collins, one of our vendor representatives, took me to lunch, and explained the art of selling. He said my job was to position myself as a resource, a service provider. As a sales professional, I could add more value by fully understanding my clients needs before recommending my product as a solution. What I did not realize until later, was that Larry was adding value to my company by teaching the sales team how to sell. He saw the need for sales mentoring, knowing that I might turn around and sell a product that was in direct competition with his line. Larry was focused on adding value first, and making a sale second. Larry was enriching the world, by teaching one sales person at a time.

Over the years, I have studied successful sales people, business leaders, customer service representatives, and a host of others who wear the name "employee." I've discovered they all carry the stone of 'value' in their pouch. When giants present a challenge, these successful people quickly slip the stone into their sling and aim true.

One of my all time heroes is Jim Rohn, America's Greatest Business Philosopher. I've listened to his tapes hundreds of times. While driving between appointments, I popped in one of Jim's tapes and heard something that caught me off guard. Jim said:

"Work harder on yourself than you do on your job. If you work hard on your job, you'll make a living. If you work hard on yourself, you'll make a fortune."

I began to reflect and review the hard work I've done. Sure, I studied in college; sure, I gave my employer more than a full day's work. Sure, I loved my wife and my children. Yet, his words continued to ring in my head. How do I work hard on myself? What can I do to improve my skills and abilities? I began to study and research the things I am passionate about. I love sales and entrepreneurship. I started reading all the books I could find on these subjects. I listened to tapes of people who were successful in sales and business. I began to pay more attention to my clients and their business strengths. I asked questions, took notes, and asked more questions. I was beginning to work harder on myself. I was beginning to add value. Then I met David Bloomfield.

David I. Bloomfield answered the ad I placed in the Wall Street Journal. At the time, I was the National Sales Manager for Unilearn, a Portland, Oregon based startup company creating interactive video learning systems. I was looking for independent sales people, Knowledge Agents, to help launch an exciting new interactive video-training product. David faxed me his resume and proceeded to use our toll-free number to hunt me down. He began to wear out our receptionist and other staff members with his calls. His messages were always short and to the point; "This is David I. Bloomfield, did you read my resume? When can I have an interview?" I admired and valued his bulldog spirit.

When I finally returned his calls, he said, "Do you know what the 'I' in David I. Bloomfield stands for? IMPATIENT!" I knew this guy was going to lead us into new and uncharted territory. I flew down to Los Angeles from Portland, Oregon to meet the impatient David I. Bloomfield. His resume seemed strong; he was passionate about selling, and wanted to learn this new technology. We agreed to meet at his favorite coffee shop for the interview. Outside the restaurant, a car pulled up. The gentleman that stepped out of then car was elderly by my standards, probably in his 70's. I watched him enter and scan the room, looking for someone he planned to meet. There were only a handful of people in the room. He saw me and walked right over. "Hello, I'm David I. Bloomfield, you must be Curt Tueffert." My mind went blank. This is David I. Bloomfield? This is the guy that will break open the Los Angeles market? Can he even lift the equipment? The fire in his eyes and the passion in his voice removed any doubt in my mind. Here I was, a 32-year-old National Sales Manager interviewing a guy that was in his seventies. David said one more thing that cleared my head of any doubt, "I'm 73 years old and dyslexic. I feel like I am 37!"

David did break open new accounts and taught me the value in adding value. David's selling career started door-to-door, selling kitchen utensils back in the 1940's and 50's. He devoted his life to sales and this profession rewarded him with a rich and full life. David would say, "Curt, try and understand what the customer needs first. Always give them honor and respect. Always treat them with kindness, even when they don't buy. And never, ever, ever, give up!" Jim Rohn said if you work harder on yourself than on your job, you'll make a fortune. Part of that fortune is money; part of that fortune is the value you have added wherever you have been, and the value you've added by the lives you have touched.

David Bloomfield came out of retirement to join my team, once again to add value and to learn something new. The value he added was his teachable spirit, always learning, always applying. What I lacked in sales technique, David had. What he lacked in technical knowledge, I provided. We made a great team.

Where can you add value?

- **Sales people** – Learn better listening skills. Learn to ask better questions. Seek first to understand and then continue seeking to understand. Make a commitment to excellence in your sales career. Find your passion and blend that into your career. Each of these actions adds value.

- **Business Leaders** – Get to really know the people you lead. Take steps today to develop their leadership skills. Invest in their future by learning more about leadership, time management, organization, process management, and encouragement. Teach these skills to your team.

- **Customer Service Representatives** – Really listen to your customers. When listening to the customer, focus on being there, with them and tuning out all the other distractions that can cause you not to really listen. To better serve your customer, take notes, when applicable.

By taking notes, you are communicating that their question, problem, or challenge is important to you. Important enough that you are writing it down. Strive for excellence by assisting them when they need help. Ask a few questions to draw them out and to see the challenge from their point of view. Become empathetic and passionate about solving their problems. Make their day and add value.

- **Parents** – Invest in seminars, books, and tapes that will help you in your parenting skills. There are many great programs that help parents, including Growing Kids Gods Way, literature from Focus On The Family, and hundreds of web sites to assist parents from toddlers to teenagers. Interview other partners, peers, grandparents, and others about their parenting styles. Become teachable to new ideas that will help you connect with your children. Schedule a date night with your children to spend individual time with them.

- **Teachers** – Get passionate about the subjects you are teaching. Your passion will ignite your students to new thoughts, ideas, and actions. Remember that you have the privilege of communicating wisdom and knowledge to the next generation. Get creative with your teaching style and with the subject matter you teach. Do something different in your class to make your point. Give your students something to remember.

The more value we add in the jobs we do and the people we touch, the less giant slaying we'll be required to perform. Not every giant in your life will have the impact that Goliath had over King Saul. Yet, every giant can be faced when you have 'Value' in your pouch; value that can reach beyond your boundaries and extends into the lives of others.

Putting Stone #4 (Value) Into Action

- Take a moment and write down all the areas in your life where you can add value.

- What three things can you do today to begin adding more value? Does it demand study and research? Does it require a time commitment? Does it require a price to pay? If it is worth it, do it today.

- Write down two people that would benefit from your commitment to add value in their lives.

- Commit to three things you can do to add more value to their lives.

Chapter 6 - Stone #5 – Confidence

"Confidence, with it you're invincible, without it; invisible." - Anonymous

David's ability to defeat this giant could not have succeeded without confidence. The situation demanded that he rely on his own abilities, fueled by his passion to serve God. David had a vision of victory, he knew the value he could bring, and he was assured his commitment to excellence through repetitive practice would not fail him.

Where is your confidence? Giant slaying requires a high degree of confidence! While building my career, there were times I lost the sale due to lack of confidence.

As the product manager for a national wholesale computer distributor, I was asked to present my business plan for the coming year during our fourth quarter review. Being in charge of $6 million in computer hardware, I slaved over the historical sales, the projections for the coming year, and my detailed plans to exceed all expectations. I rehearsed the presentation, memorized the projected increase in sales, and compared my forecasts with other product managers. I knew my numbers, but not my audience. As I walked into the room, I quickly took an executive inventory. Sitting with tired and frustrated looks where the CEO, CFO, CIO, VP of Sales, VP of Marketing, and the Human Resource Manager.

This was a tough crowd, weary from reviewing numbers most of the day. As I began with my first slide, the VP of Sales quickly cut me off. "Curt, we're running late, give us your forecasts and projections now! And tell us your plans for reducing inventory levels." I had the attention of the whole room, and no confidence. I stumbled through the required answers and left quickly, leaving a less than confident mark in their minds. I knew my stuff, yet I failed to communicate it with confidence. That meeting cost me a great deal of respect as most of the senior management questioned my ability to do my job based on that initial presentation. Fortunately I got their confidence back by working hard and doing just what I said I would do, showing them how the numbers worked out.

When you have confidence, things tend to go your way. As the National Sales Manager for Unilearn, I focused on the Fortune 200 Training and Development managers. Our product was an interactive video system that created courseware from videotape. It was revolutionary at the time, and my job was to get orders while the product was still in development. The more initial orders I got, the more this motivated the venture capital community to take an active interest in our company. Future funding was based on the acceptance of this product (concept) in the minds of the prospects and customers.

We held executive briefings across the country at airport Marriott hotels. Our direct mail and telemarketing campaigns brought in the decision makers. The right people were at the right place, at the right time. However, time and cash were running out. We needed the pre-commitments now to secure another round of funding. As the executives were filling their coffee mugs and finding their seats, the VP of Sales/Marketing pulled me aside. He reminded me of my passion for learning. He praised my commitment to excellence, and reminded me of our vision for education. I was in the zone where nothing I did could go wrong! During that presentation my confidence was at an all time high. I knew the product was right, our purpose was right, and my vision was right. I gave the presentation 110% of my effort and enthusiasm. Reports were passed back to our corporate office of our favorable impressions and second appointments were secured. We got the second round of funding; things went our way! Why? They trusted my high level of confidence. I communicated trust and confidence. That's what they needed.

The story is told of Moses and his request to explore the land of Canaan, which God had promised the Israelites. Moses selected 12 men for this reconnaissance mission. The order was quite accurate:

"Go up to the Negev and on into the hill country. See what the land is like and whether the people who live there are strong or weak, few or many. What kind of land do they live in? Is it good or bad? What kind of towns do they live in? Are they unwalled or fortified? How is the soil? It is fertile or poor? Are there trees on it or not? Do your best to bring back some of the fruit of the land." (Numbers 12:17-20 NIV)

After 40 days, all 12 men returned from the exploration trip. When asked to provide a summary, 10 men said the land is filled with powerful people, giants even! "Hey, the land may flow with milk and honey, but we'll be crushed by the giants! They are so big, we seem like grasshoppers in their eyes!" Can't you just hear their whining with the lack of confidence?

Joshua and Caleb were on the same reconnaissance mission. Same people, same land, same cities. They saw things a bit different. They had confidence, fueled with passion and forged with vision! Caleb said it best "We should go up and take possession of the land, for we can certainly do it." Why did Joshua and Caleb see things differently? They had confidence that God would provide what they needed. He did it before, he could do it again. I think vision also played a huge part in their confidence. God promised them a land and He painted a pretty good picture of what that would look like. Joshua and Caleb had the vision stone and the stone of confidence. Nothing was going to stop them from fulfilling their mission and providing an accurate report to Moses.

If you want to slay giants in your life, you need confidence. So, how do you get it? I have found these 5 steps helpful to gain confidence for slaying giants.

1. **Reflect.** Go back in time; reflect on the victories in your career, your business, your relationships, and your achievements. Capture those lessons learned and repeat them. Play them over and over in your mind. By doing this, you'll get into that state where you felt your successes. Subconsciously, you are building confidence by reliving the steps you tool and what it was like to win.

2. **Write**. Buy a notebook. Journal these victories to create vivid images of your success. What were the sounds, the sights, and even the smells? Was it hot or cold, day or night? What did you do to win? What were your emotions? Paint the sharpest picture you can.

3. **Learn**. Develop new skills. You might be unsure at first, yet over time, improvement shows itself. You must be teachable to new and creative methods. You are never too old to learn.

4. **Practice**. Hone the art and skills you need. Do it over and over again, each time, creating a small improvement.

5. **Teach**. To really be confident in a task, you need to teach it to someone else. By teaching, you see areas where you can improve, where you can touch lives in other ways.

I teach Introduction To Sales and Advanced Professional Selling at the University of Houston. When I was asked to teach sales skills, I knew I lacked the confidence. There is a passion inside me that wanted to teach; yet I lacked the excellence or the confidence. How was I going to teach at the University level? I was missing a few stones! I began at step one; reflect.

Reflect. I reflected on my selling career. I reviewed almost 19 years of sales wins, losses, success and failure. I was quick to dwell on the losses and the failure. Through discipline, I began to focus on the successes. I saw myself in those early years of sales. I felt the excitement of closing a deal. I could hear the clapping hands of my peers, congratulating me on a new sale. I saw myself as a sales manager, encouraging a frustrated sales person who just lost a sale. I saw myself giving sales presentations to small and large groups. I could feel the confidence building.

Write. I went out and bought a cheap notebook, and wrote down these experiences. I wrote my sales wins. I wrote about completing a marathon. I wrote of ties with my family and how much they mean to me. I wrote of private victories where only I saw the valor and honor in besting giants in my life. By writing them down, I relived them all over again. This was exciting; I began to think I really could pull this off!

Learn. I began to read *Customer Centered Selling* (Rob Jolles), the book issued for the course. I read it, made notes, read it again, and made more notes. Making notes was easy. Understanding the author's point of view was more challenging. I made notes where I agreed and were I disagreed with the author. His style of selling was similar to mine, yet differences appeared. I created outlines and supported the lessons with other material.

Practice. I contacted Rob Jolles, the author of the *Customer Centered Selling*, and peppered him with questions. He understood my fear and doubt and assured me that practice was the only cure for my lack of confidence in his material. So I committed to practice his sales techniques with my sales team. The more I practiced, the easier it was to use his ideas and see the results. My sales team enjoyed the new ideas as well. My confidence meter was rising.

Teach. The first semester was a test of my teaching ability. The students did not know I was a "first timer" with the course material. Think of the credibility I would have lost if they knew this was my first time! My confidence level was very present during my first semester teaching at a university. My passion for the students and the material, the commitment to excellence, the vision for their future selling careers, and the value I was both getting and giving made for a great semester.

Confidence is often elusive; seldom can we secure it with both hands. Yet, we've all been there before. We've felt confidence coursing through our veins, causing our chest to beat a little louder, giving us the air of invincibility. So, bring on the giants now!

Putting Stone #5 (Confidence) Into Action

- Confidence, with it you're invincible, without it; invisible. Where in your life are you lacking confidence? Where in your life are you very confident? What caused you to be confident?

- Reflect on the victories in your life. Where did you win, succeed, go for it, and feel really alive?

- Write down those times and the feelings that come from those positive times.

- Learn new skills that will give you more confidence. Leadership? Management? Sales? Parenting? Playing the guitar? Cooking? Gardening? Sailing?

- Practice the fundamentals required to increase your skill levels.

- Teach these newly acquired skills to others, thus, enforcing their value and confidence in you.

Chapter 7 - 5 Stones For Slaying Giants...In Sales

Sales professionals face giants daily. They may come in the form of sales quotas, difficult customers, elusive prospects, fierce sales objections, or the lack of motivation. Giants are all around us.

Now that you know the five stones for slaying giants, where do you apply them in sales? From one sales professional to another, let me say, you can, you will, you must apply them in order to improve your ability to sell.

Stone #1 – Passion In Sales

I work with many sales people in various stages of their selling career. I've talked with many sales managers about the secret ingredient of sales winners. My conclusion is that sales winners, sales professionals on the top of their game, and the top of their quotas, share this in common; *Passion*.

Charles Wesley said it best,

"Catch on fire with enthusiasm and people will come from miles to watch you burn."

Another word for passion is enthusiasm. This enthusiasm fuels your ability to overcome sales objections and all the other roadblocks sales professionals face. Passion gives you a sense of purpose, or mission to serve your clients and grow your business. When this enthusiasm burns bright, others will be attracted to you based on your genuine love of the game.

In my college years, I was a software developer for Oakleaf. The market was automotive dealerships and our software helped to automate the process of calculating payments, processing the paperwork, and getting the loan approved. I had a dual role; develop the software and provide the training. Periodically, I had the chance to train our sales people and other employees who needed to know how the software worked.

Our Vice President of Sales, Don Jackson, approached me before a training session. I'll never forget his words, "Curt, remember that you represent the finest product in the business. When you are training, you are selling. If you are passionate about our product, the class will catch that fire." That was my first exposure to the idea that I was selling from the training room. He was right. The more I taught with passion and excitement, the deeper the impact to the class and the more sales we continued to get from additional software modules.

This passion has to be genuine. It's been said that the "C" in CLOSER is for "conviction." Without the "C" of conviction, you will be a LOSER. I have used this analogy with many sales professionals and managers. How many times have we encountered a sales person who is "going through the motions?" You know the type, they are physically present, yet mentally absent from the sales call. Why does this happen? I believe they have lost either their passion for selling as a career, or they no longer believe in the company/product they represent.

Jim is a car salesman for family run dealership in North Carolina. I met Jim in January of 2001 when I spoke at a breakfast meeting. Jim is unique in two ways. First, he had been in this business for close to 20 years. Second, he had been at this particular dealership all those years. I had to know his secret. What kept him at this company when statistically, the turnover in automotive sales people are higher than average?

I asked Jim for his secret, the key to 20 years selling cars for the same dealership. His answer came quickly, "Curt, when I make a sale to a customer, I know I have a chance to sell to their family and friends, too. I love what I do and show it to all my customers. When that customer leaves, they tell their family and friends about my service and my passion." I asked Jim why this dealership. He said they have treated him right for all these years. The family who runs these stores treats their people right, based on a passion they have to treat everyone right.

The key here is to be passionate about why you are in the profession of sales. The more you treat yourself and others right, the more passionate you'll get. So, catch yourself on fire with passion and your selling influence will burn.

Stone #2 – Excellence Is Sales

Passion is one side of the balance; a commitment to excellence and continual learning is the other side. Jim Rohn once said,

"Motivation alone is not enough. If you have an idiot and you motivate him, now you have a motivated idiot."

I have seen many sales people who are very passionate about their career in sales. They love the company and the products they sell. Yet, they still remain in the middle of the pack when looking at sales performance. Why are they not at the top of the list? They have not made a commitment to improving their sales technique or their sales ability.

Teresa loved her job. She sold computer hardware and software to value added resellers and dealers. Teresa would often come in early and stay late. Her customers were in other states and she sold over the phone. She had passion and enthusiasm for the job, yet she never ranked in the top 15% of sales people for the company.

Teresa asked me what she could do to get to the top. I sensed she was frustrated with her performance and I knew she wanted the extra commissions that came from selling more. I knew where this was going, so I asked her about her enthusiasm for the job. She agreed that she loved the company, the customers, and the products she sold. We agreed her problem was not in her passion to sell.

I asked Teresa what sales book she last read. Silence. I asked her to name the top three books in her library on selling or self-improvement. Again, no answer. Teresa understood that a commitment to excellence was required to make it into the top sales club. She agreed and we began a program of reading and studying sales techniques and ideas that would help in qualifying our customers and asking more questions to better understand their needs. Teresa quickly went from being a source for products to a resource to help expand her customer's business.

Sales excellence requires discipline and study. It requires learning new tools, practicing them, and teaching them to others. It requires a desire to improve and the willingness to pay the price. Winners pay a price others (losers) will not pay. Sadly, the price is often so small.

Stone #3 – Vision In Sales

In sales, there are two types of vision. There is a personal vision, where you see yourself going and how you plan on exceeding your personal goals in sales. The second vision is what customers want and sees for themselves. I believe the more we begin to see how important this vision is, the faster our sales numbers will improve.

Your personal vision affects your drive. What will it look like when you attain your goal? What is motivating you to move forward? I met Jason when he graduated from the Excellence in Selling program at the University of Houston. I was building a new sales team at Jones Business Systems and needed strong talent willing to take a risk. Our new sales team was to promote products in the Linux market. Linux was a new operating system that competed with just about everyone because it was free, a simple download off the Internet. Jason met or exceeded everything I was looking for. Jason's personal vision was to earn a six-figure income before he turned 30. He knew it would take hard work and focus. Jason would hit the phone hard, making 50 – 70 calls, creating a super nova of energy. His goal was to close business and make money. I respected his commitment to his personal vision and to obtaining the tools and techniques to reach his goal. Jason left Jones Business Systems and landed at a Houston based software technology company where he quickly became one of the top three sales people. Recently, I've asked Jason to speak to the classes I teach at the University of Houston. His drive and determination prove you can do it when you have a clear vision.

Without a personal vision, a sale becomes just a job. Without a personal vision, you become something less than what you can be. Without a direction, any direction will do, including reverse. If you have lost your vision, work hard on getting it back. Take the right inventory and gather your resources to fight the urge to be average.

A strong personal vision is half the equation. The other half is a vision for your customer's success. Many sales people lack the ability to see where the customer is coming from. They fail to see the business transaction from the customer's point of view. To be a sales professional, you have to see how your product or service fits into your customer's vision. Where are they going, what business needs do they have? Are they in a crunch mode, or growth mode? Can they see how you can impact their vision? Often, you have to help your customers see their vision with the help of your products and services.

One of my clients is a large electronics distributor, who does business all over the world. Their sales staff operates on staggered shifts to handle the International clients. My goal was to sell them an assessment to show the objective strengths and weaknesses of their sales teams. This assessment tool would benefit them in many ways, based on our conversations and my understanding of their sales process.

What I was lacking was understanding their vision. I had difficulty communicating the impact of my services on their sales vision.

During the sales call, I knew the direction of our conversation was not going well. I began to ask more questions about the owner's selling philosophy. I wanted to know how he built this business. Then I wanted to know the role his sales managers played in sales generation and sales motivation. That is when I saw a chance to understand their vision and how I might help.

I asked permission to show the owner a sample assessment. The assessment highlighted an individual's keys to motivation and management. I pointed to the areas where selling strengths and weakness where measured. I then tied that to how the owner built this company from the ground up. If he had a tool like this, would he have been successful faster? If his sales managers had this type of objective data on their sales teams, would they be more effective managers? They were beginning to see the impact on their sales vision and the increased effectiveness of their sales managers. They gave me a chance to prove myself and make the sale.

Stone #4 – Value In Sales

If you have been in sales for any length of time, you understand the term "value add." It is what we offer in addition to our company, products, and services. If we did not have any value in the marketplace, our products would not sell. This is not the value I am talking about.

Giants in our life challenge us on our ability to sell. These giants hold us down by diminishing our value, which prevents us from expanding our ability to influence and add genuine value. Our value increases when our sales ability increases. We'll slay more giants when our value increases in the eyes of our customers and the people we serve. When we set out to increase our worth, our demand in the marketplace increases.

To increase your value you need to work on these 3 areas:

1. **Networking**. The new cliché in networking *is "it's not who you know, rather who knows you."* What do people know you for? When you increase you value, people seek you out. Networking is the vehicle for you to meet other people who know people that would be interested in your value. The more you give in networking, the more you will get back. We often forget this when we are shouting our value to people who are not interested. First get to know them and understand their business and vision, and then seek ways to help them obtain their vision, goals and objectives. This is how you add value in networking.

2. **Increase Your I.Q.** (*Influence Quotient*). Sales professionals of high value are always studying, reading, researching. They are making themselves more valuable in the marketplace. When in a selling situation, the sales professional with more influence is the one that offers better solutions. How did they make the sale? They knew more about their client, their competition, and their company's products and services. They influenced the sales in ways you could not.

3. **Give Back**. When was the last time you gave back to the community? You have a wealth of knowledge on your industry. You study the trends, the market, your products, and your competitors. There are groups of people who want to know what you know. Speak at a local networking function or civic group. Give back some of that knowledge. People in the audience will respect you and your influence will grow. Often, there are people in the audience who can refer you to others you need to meet. This is a great way to make you more valuable.

Stone #5 – Confidence In Sales

"Timid sales people have skinny kids" is an old cliché about confidence. Many a giant has won the battle, defeating sales people by taking away their confidence. If the lion is the king of the jungle, what happened to the lion in the Wizard of OZ? He lacked courage. Courage and Confidence are linked together.

Back when I was selling the interactive video product at Unilearn, I presented to many training and development managers at Fortune 500 companies. That was easy compared to one sales call to one person in San Diego, CA.

I had been cold calling from a list. I targeted San Diego because it was my favorite place and by booking appointments, I could travel from Portland, Oregon, to San Diego in the middle of Portland's gloomy season. I came across Brian Tracy International and knew this was the one and only Brian Tracy. I was relentless in trying to get the sales manager to speak with me. 14 voice mails and I was still not giving up. I flew down to San Diego, determined to meet the sales manager, and eventually Brian Tracy himself.

Without an appointment, I walked into that office and asked to speak with Pat, Brian Tracy's sales manager. "No madam, I do not have an appointment. I flew down from Portland Oregon on the hope that Pat would take pity on me and hear what I have to say." Pat must have recalled the 14 voice mails and did have pity on me. I asked for 10 minutes to explain the idea and how it would impact Brian's ability to influence people (remember the customer's vision.) After 25 minutes, I had an appointment to meet Mr. Brian Tracy himself, along with his 4 regional managers 3 weeks later.

During that time, I read all of Brian's books and listened to most of his tapes. I had Passion, Excellence, Vision, and Value. I was ready. I was confident in my ability to represent my company and the product. I flew down to San Diego on a mission to close this deal and add Brian Tracy to the list of pre-launch customers.

When I drove into the parking area, I lost all my confidence. It was as if Goliath and his four brothers were in the car taunting me. "Who do you think you are? You think you can sell? You used to live here and now you're stuck in Portland? Loser, loser, loser." This was not supposed to happen. After all, I've been in other presentations with other VIP types. I felt that I was unworthy to sell. My thoughts were jumbled. I doubted my very existence as a sales person. Immediately, I thought…"*Perhaps a new career serving flavored coffees is more my talent?*"

When I arrived, Pat, the sales manager told me which room was set up for me. She said that Brian was really excited to see this and so were his 4 regional directors. She mentioned that Brian was running late, and not to start without him. Oh, great, just what I need, a bunch of prospects excited about seeing my product and me!

The moment arrived and I could not have been any lower on the confidence scale. ***"Fake it til you make it!"*** was all I could repeat. So I began. Seven minutes into my demo, Brian cuts me off. "Curt, I appreciate you've read my books and listened to my tapes, that is apparent in your presentation style. How 'bout you being you instead of you being me?" The thought crossed my mind to take a break, walk directly to my car and never to return again. Since I was in San Diego, Mexico was just across the border, I planned my escape.

Then, the strangest thing happened, my confidence came back in waves, like the surf crashing outside the window. Mr. Brian Tracy crossed his legs, and when I looked down, I noticed he had a hole in the sole of his shoe. I caught myself staring and thought; "Brian Tracy is a mere mortal. He puts his pants on one leg at a time, and also his shoes." Yet, my shoe does not have a hole in the sole. Brian Tracy was a regular guy. With this revelation, my confidence returned.

After that, I launched into my product pitch. I knew the impact it would have on Brian's audiences, which in turn would impact more people. This product could help to communicate his message in new and creative ways by allowing his video tape series to imbed testing and immediate feedback to the person viewing his material. When the demonstration and Q&A session was over, we agreed to test one of his tapes and I was heading out the door. Pat, the sales manager came over and congratulated me on a fine presentation and said that my persistence and confidence in my product paid off. Giants lay dead all around me.

Putting The 5 Stones Into Action For Sales Professionals

- My experience with sales professionals is that they tend to loose passion over the length of their sales career. As it relates to sales, what three things can you get more passionate about?

- Sales professionals seldom get all the process training they need to enhance their sales ability. Plenty of product training, limited process training. As your strive for excellence, what four things can you do to grow? What books can you read (or reread)? What tape series can you invest in? What seminar would give you fresh tools, tips, and techniques to grow your ability to become excellent?

- Remember what I said about vision? What is your sales plan? Where are you going? What is your progress? If there is no hope for the future, there is no power in the present. Take time now to focus your vision for your sales career, sales growth, and impact. Now, what is the vision of your customer? The best way is to find out, then writes it down. Commit to them to share that vision and to help your customer get what they want.

- Sales professional, where do you add value? What is your unique value-add component? Write down the five ways you add value and commit to continued learning to further add value.

- Take a few minutes and write down your plan for gaining confidence. Reflect, Write, Learn, Practice, Teach (to others). Commit to working your plan to gain the confidence you need to move forward.

Chapter 8 - 5 Stones For Slaying Giants...In Customer Service

Customer Service in America is at an all time low. Instead of working harder to improve our customer service skills, we've settled for something less, hoping to make it up in the higher volumes of customers we serve. We should all strive to increase our customer service skills. So, why do we fail in customer service? I believe there are giants who have infiltrated our standards for customer service. These giants have substituted laziness and apathy for responsiveness and quality of work. It is easier to run and hide from these giants than to fight. Where is our David to slay these giants? Let me give you 5 stones that can increase your customer service skills, inspire your employees to greater action, and turn ranting customers into raving fans.

Henry Ford said it best; *"You can fire everyone in the company, from top to bottom, simply by deciding to shop somewhere else."* These are powerful words delivered by one of America's greatest business leaders. So, how can we strive to increase our level of customer service using the 5 Stones?

Stone #1 – Passion In Customer Service

One of the greatest examples of passion I've seen of companies and their customers is in the airline industry. I travel all across the US and use many different airlines to get from here to there. Southwest Airlines always comes to the top of the list when we discuss customer service. Jim Jacobus, the president of Champion Education Resources, illustrates this in his workshop, *WOW! Customer Service*. In researching Southwest Airlines, Jim observed that the reason they are on the top of the list is that passion starts at the top and works its way down to every employee. Southwest employees are on a mission to serve their customers. We might not like the seating arrangements or the food selection (peanuts), yet they are out to delight the customer every chance they get. This effort is seen on their faces, in their voices, and on their balance sheet.

How does one company create these raving fans while another turns customers away with their lack of passion? Ken Blanchard and Sheldon Bowles wrote the book *Raving Fans*. The book is written like a story with three main points. One of the points is:

Deliver What The Customer Wants – Deliver Plus One

First you have to know what the customer wants. That requires a great deal of passion to really, I mean REALLY, discover what they are looking for in service, speed, price, value, people, etc. Then, state the authors, deliver one percent more! After all your careful research in knowing what they desire, give it to them, plus one more percent of effort, which will exceed their expectations. There are other companies who are leaders in customer service; Marriott, Ritz Carlson, American Express, Hertz, and Starbucks have used this principle and remain very successful.

In order for this to really impact your business, employees, and customers, the buy in for outrageous customer service must come from the very top of the organization. Passion is in the hearts of many customer service representatives. Passion can lie deep with the employees that connect directly to the customer. Then, it can begin to dilute as you go higher in the organization. Day to day business, bottom lines, and *administrivia* seem to replace the passion to serve the customer. This is tragic. If we want to reclaim our desire to provide better than average customer service, we need to create raving fans from the president on down. When it flows top down and bottom up inside the corporation, then it will flow with genuine sincerity out onto the prospects and customers we have worked so hard to keep in the first place.

Another secret to great customer service is hiring people with passion to begin with. We get so wrapped up in other tangible job skills and qualifications that we forget to look into the area of passion. Many companies, including Southwest Airlines, Digital Consulting, and Marriott look for a "family fit." Meaning, would this person fit in our family, our culture, and do they share our passion for customer service? Employers can use probing questions to dig deeper into the candidate and see what they are made of. The use of assessments and other objective tools can show traits and behavioral styles that are in alignment with the proper customer service skills required. Also, when multiple team members interview the candidate, a general feeling (gut check), complimented with the objective data will uncover the degree of passion to customer service.

In offering WOW! Customer Service workshops we stress that:

Front-line employees will treat customers only as good as management treats front-line employees.

This passion has to be congruent in all levels of staff and management in order for it to be genuine. At Nordstom's, the famous department store, known for excellence in customer service, they have two types of employees. Those who serve the customer and those who serve those who serve the customer. The whole idea and attitude of service is portrayed throughout the whole company in only two types of employees. The customer knows this, feels this, and sees this as they interact with the Nordstrom's staff.

Stone #2 – Excellence In Customer Service

The book, Raving Fans, starts with a simple point; *Decide What You Want.* Decide what level of customer service you plan to give through your company and through your department. Then decide on what level of service you plan to give to your customers. The key to making this a successful program is striving for the excellence once you know the level of service you plan to offer. Once you can define it, you can strive for it.

Carl Sewell owns a string of automotive dealership in Dallas, Texas and other cities. He has built his business on the ideas of superior customer service. Sewell Village Lexus/Cadillac has been successful when other dealerships were wringing their hands in panic. When some dealerships where treating the customer as something other than king, Sewell was creating customers for life. This philosophy has proven so successful that Carl Sewell wrote the book; *Customers For Life*.

There is a price to pay when you decide you want superior customer service. For the Sewell dealerships, that price is training and education. The Sewell family of dealerships offers many training classes, including WOW! Customer Service. Each employee is required to participate in this 6-hr class. Since customer service excellence starts with deciding what you want, training is required to gain the edge. The class covers areas such as handling angry customers, 7/11 rule of first impressions, knowing just who the customer is, communication traits, and moments of truth. The strongest part of this course is understanding Behavioral Styles when working with customers. The employees who serve the customer are taught how to spot their Behavioral Style and offer superior customer service by communicating value based on their style.

Stone #3 – Vision In Customer Service

The key to customer service success is to see service through the eyes of the customer. What do they expect? What do they see when they are standing in line? What do they hear when calling about an issue? The more we know about our customers and what they want, the quicker we can create an experience that they will appreciate and remember.

How did Marriott and Nordstrom's become household names for superior customer service? They spent a lot of time listening to the voices of their customers. It was their customers who gave them the vision as to what superior customer service is. To understand what great customer service is, you have to ask the customer what they expect. Only then can you begin to build a sharp vision on what your company can offer. Remember that it is not about you, it is about them and their needs, wants and desires. Companies with strong vision constantly ask their current and former customers "What re we doing right, doing wrong, and how can we change to better serve you?"

One great story of vision comes from a guest representative from Marriott. He received a call from a frantic bride-to-be who was trying to schedule a honeymoon at one of the Marriott resorts in the Caribbean. The dates fell under the "black-out" period for the resort. Black-out periods are dates restricted to special offers, usually in the high demand seasons. To make matters more challenging, the fiancé had just been diagnosed with brain cancer with only a few months to live. Sadly, the call ended when the bride-to-be could not find a solution to the blackout dates, thanked the Marriott guest representative, and hung up.

The Marriott employee was very moved by the call. So moved he called the General Manager of the Marriott Caribbean resort and explained the tragic situation. The GM not only understood and saw the vision of the situation; he overrode the restrictions, placed them in a room and gave the couple a free room upgrade. When the guest representative called the anxious bride-to-be, she was thrilled at first, and then proceeded to tell the Marriott employee that the airlines could not get the couple to the resort during that scheduled week. Still keeping Vision (for the customer) in the front of his mind, the Marriott employee called the airlines, which did not have a frequent flier relationship with Marriott. He explained the tragedy of the upcoming wedding, the honeymoon, and the diagnosed brain cancer with a limited life sentence.

The airlines saw the vision of superior customer service and rewrote the rules for this couple. Not only did they allow for flying during that period, they upgraded them to first class and paid for the tickets! Not to be outdone, Marriott also comped the couple for the upgraded room. *(The Spirit To Serve*, J.W. Marriott Jr. & Kathi Ann Brown)

Do all customer service stories with vision have to be that dramatic? No. What they require is a business culture of vision. They require a superior vision for what the customer needs and the ability to go beyond the norm and get it done. This vision comes from the top down, from management's ability to create and feed the vision. This vision also comes from the bottom up, with pride in working for a customer driven company, representing a high quality product or service, and the respect for each person who works to enhance the vision.

Stone #4 – Value In Customer Service

When I talk about Value in customer service, I mean two things; the value the company places in serving the customer, and the value the customer sees in being served. Webster's New World Dictionary defines value as:

> *That quality of a thing according to which it is thought of as being more or less desirable, useful, estimable, important, etc. That which is desirable or worthy of esteem of its own sake; thing or quality having intrinsic worth.*

The value of customer service can be seen from both sides of the equation. One side is the customer who places value on how they are treated by the employees, their place in the selling process, their request when things are in question, and their treatment when things just go wrong. The other side of the equation is the value the company places on the customer, from the initial gaining of the customer, to the quality of the product or service offered, to the nurturing of the relationship once the business transaction is completed. Contained on both sides of the equation are many areas where value can be esteemed or lost. There are giants to slay in the camp of the customer and in the camp of the company. Reaching for the stone of Value will help to gain superior customer service in the eyes of both the customer and the company.

William Bynam and Jeff Cox, drive the value point home in their book; *HeroZ*. These authors started writing books on empowerment starting with *Zapp! The Lightning of Empowerment*, and have continued that theme in HeroZ. The story centers on the famous Lamron Castle. The castle knights are constantly dispatched to fight pesky dragons that threaten the citizens of Lamron. Each knight uses arrows manufactured by the workers in Lamron castle. The knights are facing more dragons than ever. Many of the citizens are leaving Lamron for other cities with fewer dragons. The workers are bored with their jobs, and everything is set in pale gray, lacking any and all sense of color. All this was seen as bad news. The good news was \that Art Halegiver, one of the arrow makers, attempted a quality improvement program. Throughout the book, Art Halegiver posted notes (discoveries) regarding the building of arrows and superior customer service. While many workers might have thought of ideas to improve quality, they questioned their own ideas, so they kept them to themselves. Art wanted to see a quality improvement process so he posted his discoveries where others could read them and use them to add quality. Two of these discoveries were:

To Improve Quality Is To Improve What the Customer Values.
First Improve What's Most Important to the Customer.

Slaying Giants in customer service starts when you know what the customer values. Too often, we hold great company meetings, focusing inward, asking ourselves what do our customers value. We make a list and act on it, without first checking with the customers. This goes with the stone of Vision; knowing what the customer wants by taking the time to ask.

You can start with by using customer surveys, Internet sites, and phone calls to customers asking for their input, yet it should not end here. The second step is to visit the customer and see the impact of your product or service in the context of the customer's environment. How are they using your product? What are they using your product for? What significant impact does your product or service have on their business or quality of life?

When you invest the time to know what the customer values, then you will know where improvement is required. Ask your employees what they are hearing from the customers. Invest in the time, listen, and ask questions. Fix the next thing right and the right thing next.

As the Vice President of Sales for a large computer distributor in Houston, we faced this giant head on. Were we really adding value with our credit policies? The giant tried to prevent us from even considering the question, always stating; *If it ain't broke, don't fit it.* Somehow, a new policy was created that required each customer who purchased with a credit card to complete a written form, providing us with their proper mailing address, and other data. This new requirement was to prevent credit card fraud. In itself, this was a good policy for both the company (reduced fraud) and the customer (dishonest customers beware!). However, a new message was sent and a new discovery occurred which killed any sense of value.

The new message we communicated was **"We Do Not Trust You"** therefore; complete this form and we will begin completing your order when the necessary approvals are finished. In the quest of Quality Improvement, we lost some good customers who purchased via credit card. In hindsight, we should have communicated better why this policy was in place and ask the customers first what they thought of such a change in purchasing. After all, none of our competitors required this for credit card transactions.

Our new discovery really killed the idea of increasing value to our customers. We were located in Texas, under the Central time zone. When customers purchased via American Express, we called to the East Coast (one hour ahead) to verify all the information. This source for verification closed at 4:30pm (Eastern time), which was 3:30pm Central, and 1:30pm West Coast. Since this new policy was created inside our company in the spirit of customer service, we failed to ask what the customer valued. So, if a purchase was made after 3:30 CST, the order could not be placed or verified until the next day!

Remember Art Halegiver's discovery; *Improve What's Most Important to the Customer*? Many of our customers needed products overnight because of something breaking at their customer's site. They depended on us to ship products out based on our Central Time zone. This new policy prevented our customers (most on the West Coast), paying with American Express, to get the product they needed overnight. We lost some great customers to our competition before we listened to them and began to add their value to our business. That policy was eventually changed and we went to our customer base for their suggestions and recommendations. We began placing more value in our customer's ideas than in our internal meetings. We stopped assuming what our customers wanted.

Stone #5 – Confidence In Customer Service

What is confidence? It is a firm belief, trust and reliance. Confidence is a belief in one's own abilities. So where does confidence fit in customer service? How can you slay giants with confidence?

Remember how David told King Saul he could take on Goliath? While all the other soldiers were timid, David had a strong belief in his own abilities to win. When we as companies begin to have passion, excellence, vision, and value in our customer service offerings, confidence or a firm belief will be a natural byproduct. Another word for confidence is empowerment.

When we empower our front line employees and managers with passion, excellence, vision, and value, they become so much more confident in their ability to serve, to add value, to improve quality, and to offer new insights to improve the process again and again.

Why did the Marriott guest representative even call the General Manger of the Caribbean Resort? Wasn't that an expensive long distance phone call? He made the call because he could, plain and simple. He knew the General Manager would listen because the philosophy of empowerment and confidence is instilled in all Marriott employees.

Why did we, a high technology computer distributor, fail to create a policy with the customer in mind? Lack of confidence in our ability to create strong customer service was the diagnosis.

When faced with a customer service issue, would you rather have your company represented by a timid employee or an empowered and confident employee? I know that is too simple of a question, yet, when have we seen these striking opposites? Here are a list of places where customer service can be impacted by empowerment and confidence. At the fast food restaurant, dry cleaners, local coffee kiosk, car rental counter, airline reservations representative, hotel front desk, local hardware store, food supermarkets, automotive repair shop, fashion stores, hair dressers, schools, phone service, cable television, video rentals, etc.

The list never stops. You can slay many giants by adding passion, excellence, vision, value, and confidence to your company philosophy and customer service relationships. Once the change has begun, continue to make the small adjustments and strive for continuous, continuous improvement.

Putting The 5 Stones Into Action For Customer Service Professionals

- Working with people, especially unhappy people can drain you of passion for your job. The demands placed on customer service professionals can be stressful. What four things can you do to add passion in your job that will impact the people you work with and the customers you interact with?

- What is excellence in customer service? How do you define excellence in what you do? What are the steps you can take, today, to raise the excellence in your work with customers?

- Often when dealing with people in a customer service situation, you have to see their challenge from their perspective. You have to catch their vision of the event, the question, or the situation you are helping to resolve. How can you sharpen your focus on their vision, their level of expectation of you and the service you provide?

- As a customer service professional, how do you add value? Is it your Passion, Excellence, and Vision? Is it your ability to become empathetic to the needs of your customer? What five ways do you add value in your customer service role?

- Where are you confident most when dealing with customers? What give you that confidence? Can you improve on that and teach it to others? Make a commitment to take the five steps of gaining confidence and help someone who could use an extra dose. (Reflect, Write, Learn, Practice, Teach)

Chapter 9 - 5 Stones For Slaying Giants...In Leadership

Stone #1 – Passion In Leadership

There are many giants awaiting you in a leadership position. Giants hired to question your authority, judgment, communication, or action. Giants skilled in the art of squelching your passion by pouring gallons of water on your ideas, vision, and dreams. Giants skilled in the art of political warfare, keeping score and knowing their agenda will always be greater than yours. What single stone will assist you in slaying these giants? Passion.

When terrorists struck America on September 11, 2001 we were caught off guard. The attack awakened a passion inside the country and the citizens. It also allowed one man to show the nation his passion. President George W. Bush stepped up to the role and the call of Commander In Chief. When passion was required, he filled the gap. When strong leadership was demanded, he stepped in. In addition, his cabinet had been filled with passionate leaders in their own right.

Passion gives life and authenticity to the leader. Passion is the burning desire, the "fire in the gut" of the leader. President Bush communicated his passion visually by his expressions and his physical actions. He also communicated them verbally with the tone and inflection of his words. When you listened to President Bush's appeal to the nation that we will continue the battle against terrorists until it is finished, you got a sense of genuine commitment that comes from a source and strength called passion.

Other leaders, fictional and non-fictional show passion. Some of our earliest television personalities portrayed characters who lead with passion. Capitan James T. Kirk of the Starship Enterprise was passionate about discovering new worlds and to *"boldly go where no man has gone before."* This is a combination of both passion and vision. You knew where Captain Kirk stood on leadership and his authority role. You also knew that his crew was working as a team to achieve the overriding mission. That mantle was passed to Capitan Jean Luke Picard in Star Trek Next Generation. There were little or no doubt about who the leader of that starship was and what his mission directive was. Granted these are fictional characters, yet they support the case that passion is a critical requirement for leadership. These fictional characters and television shows translated into mega-dollars for these actors as audiences hungered for passion and leadership.

Two other examples are in the movies *Apollo 13* and *Gladiator*. Tom Hanks played the part of Astronaut James Lovell, who led the team through many earthbound exercises and drills to get them ready for the Apollo 13 mission to safely land on the moon. It was feared that one of the astronauts had the measles and needed to be scrubbed from the mission. The responsibility of delivering that message fell on Lovell and only he could deliver it. His passion for leadership, excellence, and a sense of destiny allowed him to deliver that difficult message to his crew with a sense of purpose and finality. Granted, Lovell might have agreed with the crew that there was no measles outbreak, yet he continued to take his team member off the mission and replace him with another for the safety of the mission. When the tough decisions have to be made, having a high degree of passion for what you are called to be and what you are called to do will help you make the hard decisions that often come daily.

Gladiator has been reviewed as one of the all time favorite movies for this genre of action and violence. The leadership ability of Russell Crowe playing Maximus Decimus Meridius, the general of the North Army serving Caesar, was unmistakable. His passion was to serve Rome and Rome alone. When he was not serving and fighting, he longed to return to his wife and only son, at home on the farm. Vivid images played throughout the movie, showing Maximus doing his duty and longing for his reunion with his wife and son.

During several scenes, Maximus is called to serve the Emperor as his greatest general. His passion for battlefield victory is equal to the concern of his men, who risk everything, including their lives. The battle of Germania is the final blow to the uprising against Rome, and Maximus proves his merit and skill by using battlefield strength, strategy, and his passion for leadership. Prior to battle, Maximus inspects his troops; he is concerned for the men, the equipment, and knowing each man is there fighting for the same reason, to fight the righteous fight. As he walked through the lines, you gain a sense of the passion his men have for him, and his concern for the men. "*What we do here, echoes in eternity*" states Maximus prior to the onslaught. When the emperor arrives to survey the victory, Maximus greets him. As the thousands of soldiers cheer, the cheering is really directed toward Maximus and not the emperor of Rome. Taken by surprise, and encouraged by the Emperor himself, Maximus raises his sword to signal he appreciates the cheering. You can see the passion filling the movie screen.

Has passion inspired you, the leader, to giftedness and greatness? Has passion overcome your fatigue? Has passion killed the giants battling for your role as a leader? Passion was the prerequisite for David to slay Goliath. We see that passion piqued when David answers the giant challenge with his own; "*Who is this uncircumcised Philistine that he should defy the armies of the living God?*" So much leadership potential contained in a 12 year old boy.

If you are reading this and lack the passion for leadership shown by the characters mentioned above, perhaps you need to seek Safe Places, Still Times, and Special Friends to carve out that passion. Leaders today have more demands on them than ever before. They are measured by higher standards and have little or no room for error in their lofty positions. Publicly traded companies are cycling through leaders quickly to appease the demands and standards of Wall Street and the fickle requirements of shareholders. Information Technology captains are given less and less time to implement more and more technology to feed the corporate beast.

One word of caution; Passion when unchecked can lead to obsession. Obsessive leaders tend to drive their people too hard, and loose the subtle balance between empowerment and slavery. To insure a strong drive of passion in your leadership, the other four stones, Excellence, Vision, Value, and Confidence are required. Only then can you maintain an effective balance.

Stone #2 – Excellence In Leadership

"A pile of rocks ceases to be a rock when somebody contemplates it with the idea of a cathedral in mind". Saint Exupery

Where does the excellence come from in a leader? It is worldly experience, military training, self-education, or a combination of all this and more? When leaders strive for excellence, cathedrals are built out of rocks, bridges span vast rivers and bays, diseases are cured, and companies are built to innovate or economize the current situation. Excellence requires, no, demands the use of the other four stones.

Charles Garfield's work on peak performers revealed that leaders in business, academics, and athletics require visionary purpose. Yet, without the desire for excellence, they would never have been more than average in their performance or discoveries. Taking golf as an example, Tiger Woods disciplines himself to practice every combination of easy and difficult golf strokes. He does this to perfect his swing (physical game) and his passion for excellence (mental game). In business, IBM continues to lead the world in building computers that out perform their competition. A key reason is their demand for excellence. Nobel prize winners work without sleep on their projects, requiring and demanding excellence of themselves and of their team members. And let us not forget the military. The constant repetitive drills, the routine missions, and the double and triple checking of all the equipment is for one primary purpose; excellence. When called for battle, the

US Military is #1 in the world. Why? Excellence. Just look at the Navy Seals, the Army Rangers, the Marine Green Berets, and the infamous Delta Force.

Earl Tipton and Mark Ross are the leaders of an adult Bible Study class I attend at our church here in Houston Texas. Earl committed, at an early age, to memorize large sections of scripture. His commitment to excellence in scripture memorization is truly remarkable. Mark Ross, the teacher for this class, commits many hours of preparation time prior to teaching on Sunday mornings. Hunched over many reference books, commentaries, and works by other authors, Mark strives for excellence each and every time he teaches this class. This is one example of leaders who value the merits of excellence in their leadership roles. The result is quality teaching, which gives the class members depth and insight into the lessons in the Bible.

Few people really strive for excellence. Most people see their inherent weaknesses and resolve to live with them. Areas of self-improvement and deeper learning are given a passing glance. Leaders who understand excellence also understand where it is lacking in themselves. They have the energy and desire to strengthen those areas of weakness. Demanding their own self-improvement is the hinge on which excellence in leadership swings.

Winston Churchill knew this and set a course for self-improvement. Early in his career, he was stationed in India. He had a larger portion of stubbornness than most at his early age. That stubbornness held him back from the insight of self-improvement. When he discovered this weakness, he launched into a campaign of self-education for leadership skills and to create a life he wanted through the acquisition of knowledge. In one of his communications, he wrote "I resolve to read history, philosophy, economics, and things like that…" (*Never Give In; The Extraordinary Character of Winston Churchill,* Stephen Mansfield). He enrolled in the school of self-education with Gibbon's eight-volume *Decline And Fall*, all the works of Macaulay, most of Darwin, Aristotle, Plato, and Adam Smith. At times, he would spend 4-5 hours a day committing to this self-education and striving to become excellent in his education and future role as leader. (*Pillars of Leadership*, David J. Vaughan)

What are you doing to increase your knowledge? Are you reading and researching? Often, the leader gets so busy in their day-to-day affairs and responsibilities that they stop growing. This dulls the blade of excellence and can dull the leadership senses as well. Commit yourself today to self-improvement through self-education as young Churchill did.

I discovered the value of self-improvement in my twenties. Being in sales, there was always a book to read or a tape to listen to that would offer me insight and advice. I was hungry for the knowledge and still continued to read and listen to successful leaders of industry who have the experience and proven methods which will help me improve. One of my favorite speakers is Jim Rohn, *America's Greatest Business Philosopher*. One day, while driving from one sales appointment to another, I popped in a Jim Rohn tape into my Honda's cassette player. I listened and learned from him talking about habits and excellence. His basic philosophy had three points; Learn, Practice, and Teach.

First, when striving for excellence, begin by learning something new. Learn a new business theory, a new marketing principle, or new management idea, something fresh. Second, begin putting that idea to practice. At first, you may not be very good at the execution or implementation of that new idea, tool, or technique. Yet, after committing to this practice, you'll begin to gain confidence and see the return on investment. Third, teach this to someone else. That is really where the rubber meets the road, when you communicate this new learned skill or idea to someone else and help them grasp it. You'll learn it quicker when you teach it to others.

I constantly look for new ideas, new thoughts, and new techniques. Recently, I heard someone talk about writing sales proposals and fresh closing techniques. I put both ideas into practice. I changed the way I did proposals and the way I closed business. The first few times where difficult and clunky. Then, I got some feedback from a prospect that enjoyed my proposal based on the new language and value proposition layout. I moved right into the new close and got the sale. So, I completed the Learn and Practice parts, now the teaching. As a professor at the University of Houston, I teach Introduction To Sales and Advanced Professional Selling. The timing was right and I introduced these new ideas to my class, thus completing the cycle. "Fresh" and "Useful" was the feedback I got from the students, which gave me a double return on my investment.

You might be reading this section as a business leader, educational leader, or holding a leadership role somewhere. Begin today to learn something new. Like Churchill, stop being stubborn and enroll in a self-education or self-improvement program. Learn one new thing, place it into practice, and then teach others this one new thing. Soon, that will become a habit and you'll be on your way to sharpening the sword of excellence in leadership. Now, what about vision…

Stone #3 – Vision In Leadership

Great leaders are great visionaries. Their vision is to see themselves setting the standard for the rest of the world to follow. Setting the trend, breaking the mold, doing the job better, faster, and less expensive. Sometimes it is a vision to cure a disease, to solve an unsolvable puzzle, to break a world record, to raise the bar and set the standard. Leadership and Vision go hand in hand. Vince Lombardi had vision for the Greenbay Packers. Michael Jordan for the Chicago Bulls. Moses for the Israelites, and Martin Luther King for his Freedom Rallies.

Remember the original Star Trek series? At the opening of the show, you would hear Capitan James T. Kirk stating:

> *"Space... The Final Frontier. These are the voyages of the Star Ship Enterprise. It's continuing mission: To explore strange new worlds; to seek out new life and new civilizations; to boldly go where no man has gone before."*

Captain Kirk was a leader with vision! As we have watched in many, many episodes, James T. Kirk had the vision and took his crew to the brink of destruction and back, and saved the universe on a weekly basis. Captain Picard, from *Star Trek Next Generation* continued that same tradition of strong leadership.

As the Vice President of Sales for Jones Business Systems, my job was to set a vision, to rally the sales force toward a goal, and destination. One particular quarter, we decided to set the goal for $8 million in sales for the quarter. This amount in sales had never been done in the history of the company. Sure it was a stretch, yet the responsibility fell on my shoulders. In order to get that vision from my mind to the minds of the sales professionals, we created a 6-foot thermometer and posted it at the front of the office. Everyone coming and going would see this giant thermometer and know we were out to set new records in sales. Since orders came into the office daily, we agreed to send emails out to the sales force daily with our sales progress. Weekly, we'd summarize and show our progress by updating the wall-mounted thermometer. Soon, everyone in the company, from the accounting department, tech support, product integration, and the warehouse was interested in the progress of the thermometer. "How much did we do today?" "Where do we stand?" "Are we going to make it?" We created the right buzz, and the efforts paid off. At the end of the quarter we came very close to the $8 million. We missed the $8 million goal but set 2 new records, the highest quarterly sales in history and the highest quarterly gross profit. Mission and vision accomplished.

Not every leader has a pure and positive motive for their vision. History is filled with people like Stalin, Hitler, and Osaka Bin Laden. These leaders sought the attainment of their vision through the bloodshed and destruction of innocent people. Their vision was corrupt from the start. It took a considerable amount of effort to stop these dark visions from overtaking the world. Another dark vision is profit taking from a corporation and out from under the stockholders and employees. In Houston we are still feeling the effects from Enron declaring bankruptcy and laying off thousands of workers. It would appear that a select few, held a corrupt vision of money for themselves, while the rest of the employees, and other investors lost. This loss will be felt for many years. Retirement accounts and investments devalued to the point of futile recuperation while the leaders who saw and knew the vision was corrupt, remained silent and gained sizable profits. This has been called the largest bankruptcy in US history. Enron had a passion for the energy business and excellence. Yet, I question the vision, the value and the confidence that both management and some employees had. There were corrupt practices that were illegal. There was fear of reprisal and termination, which lead to a lack of confidence in speaking your mind and alerting the right people about the corrupt business dealings. This eroded any confidence for doing was what right. And with the questionable accounting practices, the value placed on employees and their future retirement savings caused some in management to withhold the truth from the investment community and Enron employees. Passion, Excellence, Vision, Value, and Confidence are the stones needed to slay giants, both inside and outside the walls of your professional and personal life.

When David faced the Israelite army and saw they had no vision, he stepped in and provided one for Saul and all of Israel. The stakes where high, and whoever lost, would be the slaves of the conquering army. David had a vision of greatness and purpose, and was confident in what God would provide. When Saul had lost hope, David shared the story of how he killed the bear and lion to protect his sheep. This gave Saul an ounce of hope, and a sprinkling of vision. That's why he agreed to let David meet the challenge. When you have the stones of Passion and of Excellence, Vision is right there, complimenting the other two.

Have the giants in your leadership role taken your vision? Does your vision seem out of focus? Do you see yourself squinting each time you take a leadership role, wondering what's going to happen next? Think of Christopher Columbus and his vision. So many giants tried to steal it. Where would the money come from? Would the Queen of England really listen? Was there land just over the horizon? Columbus has a passion for adventure and knowledge. He strived for excellence in his self-education and self-improvement. His vision came from his mission. Not only was he out to sail around the known world, he was charged with the task to bring the Gospel to any people he met. His religious strength and conviction was also his passion and his vision. As new giants came to battle on a daily basis, Columbus drew his stones and continued to move forward. This is your challenge. This is your task. Keep your vision crystal clear. Use every means available to communicate your vision to the people you lead. Words, pictures, symbols, logos, themes, marketing, meetings, emails, web sites, everything and anything you can use to place that vision in the minds of those who require it.

Stone #4 – Value In Leadership

David Vaughn, in his book *Pillars of Leadership* states, "A true leader…exercises influence because he is a man of virtuous character, competent ability, and sacrificial service. His moral authority is both earned and deserved." (pg. 31). Leadership is proportional to the value placed on a person's character, ability, service, and authority.

How a person adds value in a leadership role can be directly linked to Vaughn's statement above. In a leadership role, you are required to add value. When that value is no longer required, the leadership role can be removed. When the value is diminished based on compromising character, ability, service, or authority, the leadership role is in peril.

A recent example is former President Clinton and his public revelation to the relationship with Monica Lewinski. As the President of the United States, a high degree of responsibility is placed on this leadership role. The citizens of the U.S. heard about lies and half-truths, sexual misconduct and impeachment proceedings. The aftermath of this was a devaluing of his ability to lead this country. Many Americans no longer saw him as an honest and upstanding President who could lead the country. They reduced his value based on his immoral behavior, his implied misrepresentation, and a lying on the witness stand. Clinton's legacy will never escape the antics that occurred in and around the White House during his term in office. His value was forever reduced, his legacy tarnished.

Another prominent figure is Rudolph Guliani, the former mayor of New York City. During the crisis of September 11th, 2001, Mayor Rudy Guliani showed the world his character, competent ability, and sacrificial service. To that end, Time magazine awarded him the honor and title of "Man Of The Year." After September 11th, giants surrounded "ground zero" and the citizens of New York. The people of New York needed value in their leadership and Guliani stepped up and united the city in their time of doubt and hurting. His appearances, communication, and character all added value to his leadership, making him truly the man of the year.

How do you add value in leadership? How does that value increase? In business, I believe value is placed on your leadership in four ways;

1. By the people serving under you
2. The experience you bring to the table
3. The excellence you continue to pursue.
4. Willingness to go the extra mile and do more than is expected.

Dwight Eisenhower once said that the mark of a great leader is that he has followers. It is these followers who place a certain value in one's leadership ability. Good or bad, you will know from the kinds of people who follow the leader. Leaders who have a high degree of value in their leadership and in the ones who follow will take others to places they would not go themselves. The goals will be stretched, the work hard, and the reward great. Followers will sacrifice, double their efforts, and get others to contribute more, simply by placing a high value on their leader.

My first "real job" after college was working for Oakleaf , a firm that developed hardware and software for the Automotive Dealerships. Working in the marketing department, the leader was John Boyd. He did not command with massive authority or overriding power. He had a gentle manner that made us all work extra hard. There were times when software deadlines demanded completion. The code needed debugging, the Q&A people needed to test, and the customers were anticipating the new release. Our group of five banded together and worked day and night to get the job done. Not because John screamed and shouted, not because he threatened but simply because he asked. And in asking, his value was almost priceless in getting a group of software developers focused on the task at hand.

What is the experience you bring to the table? Significant value is placed on leaders who come to the job with depth and a wealth of street smarts. Increase your value by becoming a leader in your industry, in your house, and in your chosen career.

Stone #5 – Confidence In Leadership

When it comes to leadership, confidence is a prerequisite and it that requires constant reflection and introspection. With confidence leaders persevere and have the tenacious desire to complete the task.

There are a great many leaders who come to mind that personify confidence. Christopher Columbus started on his journey when he was 10 years old. Through hands-on experience and self-education he acquired a masterly knowledge of mathematics, astronomy, geography, cosmography, history, and classical literature. With all his conversations and teamwork with other scholars, seamen, and saints, he was convinced and confident that the Indies could be reached by sailing west (*The Pillars of Leadership*, Vaughn)

Patrick Henry is noted as one of America's most powerful and popular patriots of the American Revolution. He had many personal failures in his life, yet refused to give up confidence in his ability to lead. As a political orator and statesman, Henry moved America forward by leading the cause for freedom and independence.

William Wilberforce was confident slavery would be defeated in his lifetime. His forty-year crusade against slavery saw its demise in 1833 and Wilberforce's book, *A Practical View*, laid the foundation for new moral highs after his death. Wilberforce was confident his quest for the abolishment of slavery would occur in his lifetime. On July 26, 1833 the Emancipation Bill passed through Parliament. 72 hours later, Wilberforce died. His confidence and perseverance had won. Calvin Coolidge, also a man of confidence and perseverance wrote:

"Nothing can take the place of persistence. Talent will not. Nothing is more common than unsuccessful men with talent. Genius will not. Unrewarded genius is almost a proverb. Education will not. The world is full of educated derelicts. Persistence and determination alone are overwhelmingly powerful."

One of my favorite leaders who inspired confidence was Sir Winston Churchill. I am sure there were times during the Nazi conflict when Churchill could have doubted his confidence in his leadership ability. He could have doubted his ability to influence the English parliament and the alliance partners he needed to defend Britain. Yet, he drew on his ability and has sense of purpose, knowing Nazism was wrong and that defeat was necessary. How would he rally the British people and army to see things his way? I believe Churchill drew upon his self-education, his previous experience, and the vision he had for his English countrymen. Hitler was wrong, this enslavement of Jews was wrong, and this movement against an Arian race was wrong. It was time to stand up and fight.

Toward the end of his life, Churchill was asked to give a speech to a newly graduating class of students. Fresh from the requirements of hard study, these elite students were ready to take on the world. They were ready to begin making their mark in time and space and to apply their new knowledge in the business world. There they sat, knowing the great Sir Winston Churchill would be delivering their graduation message and casting his reflective experience and life applications to these newly minted graduates.

Churchill arose from his seat of honor and slowly made his way to the lectern where he was to speak. Towering over the students, he gazed from left to right, front row to the back, holding the face of each student in his eyes. The students in turn, held their breath, ready to savor the words of such an elder statesman. Here was the man who delivered England from the edge of destruction. The one who faced Hitler and did not blink. The man who held confidence by his very large status.

Churchill reviewed the crowed of graduates and said; *"Never Give Up!"* The students waited, ready for the powerful insight of this great leader. Churchill held their eyes and stated again, *"Never Give Up!"* This time, with a larger dose of passion, excellence, vision, and value. The students began to see the impact, to fully understand what those words meant, cast by the master. Churchill held that phrase for just long enough, and said, *"Never, Ever, Ever, Ever Give Up!"* He then left the lectern and sat down.

Those words hit the mark. Those words impacted each of the graduates in a very personal and powerful way. In one grand motion, the students stood, clapping and cheering the great elder statesman. The ovation could be heard everywhere as Churchill delivered a message that was so powerful is could only be delivered by the slayer of giants who selected the stone of confidence.

As you read this chapter on leadership, note that confidence can be learned if you are lacking it today. Reflect on the areas of your life where you are passionate, where you have won, where you have succeeded. These are the areas where you can gain or regain your confidence. Reflect on the sounds, the sights, and the smells. Was it a small victory? How can you expand it? What part was of a team effort, what part did you play?

Now, write down those moments when you had the confidence needed to overcome the roadblocks. You see where you had confidence in the past you can recreate it again, when you need it. Many leaders use symbols to spark their need for confidence. Leaders collect pictures of eagles or have eagle statues that reflect the symbolic power and majesty of the eagle. Others choose the rhinoceros as a symbol of thick skin, power, and the stubborn way the rhino charges to break strongholds. What is your symbol? What is your touchpoint to gain confidence?

My words to you here are that of Churchill's; "Never Give Up"! Gather the required memories, the symbols, the biographies and autobiographies of other great leaders to motivate yourself forward. Listen to the tapes of other leaders and heroes teaching principles that will move you forward. Network with other leaders to hear fresh ideas and ask someone to hold you accountable. Never give up!

Confidence, with it you are invincible, without it, invisible.

Putting The 5 Stones Into Action In Leadership

- One of the elements of successful leaders is the stone of Passion. What leadership traits do you have which require additional passion? How will you gain the passion if you do not have it? List a series of action steps that you can take to gain passion in your leadership role and responsibility.

- Churchhill continued to study well into his later years. Great military leaders read and studied the battles fought long ago. What steps are you taking to create excellence in your leadership ability. What three areas could you focus on for additional excellence? What steps can you take today to move toward a higher state of excellence in these three areas?

- Leaders both have a vision and communicate that vision to the people who serve. What is your leadership vision? Can you write this down in under 5 sentences with clarity of purpose, passion and excellence? Begin today to craft a vision statement for your leadership, incorporating all that you have learned from the previous chapters.

- Leaders add value by their actions and their ability to grow additional leaders. Where are you adding value in your leadership role? What is required to add more value and to develop other leaders around you? List the five action steps required to add more value to the task at hand and the people you are developing.

- List the 4 areas where your leadership has the greatest amount of confidence. What has caused that confidence to be so strong? If you are lacking that confidence, what will it take to develop your leadership skills to a level you feel is both effective and confident? Make a list of things you can do today to grow your confidence level. Prioritize the top 5 things you can do and make your plan to grow your confidence.

Chapter 10 - Conclusion

A personal note: I hope I have helped you gain a greater understanding of Passion, Excellence, Vision, Value, and Confidence. Most of us don't have an abundance of all five stones, yet all of us have the ability to increase our portion of each.

How much does it cost to have more of these five stones? To some, the investment is minor, taking only the will and the time to gain what they have little of. For others, these stones come at a high price. Sacrifice and rethinking might be the cost to gain more of these five stones. Is it worth it? Think about this, what would King Saul have done if David had not appeared on the battlefield? It was the 40th day of battle and his troops were discouraged. Could the battle have continued or would the Philistines have overrun the camp with little to no resistance? A different outcome would have changed history.

I have seen too many companies fall to giants because they lacked these 5 stones. Recently the collapses of companies like Enron, Kmart, and Global Crossing show that giants can easily overtake you if you and your company are not prepared. For individuals, I have seen people settle for just being average, when they could have had more if they fought with these five stones. They lacked the Passion, Excellence, Vision, Value, and Confidence needed to win, to reach their goals, and to be really alive, to take a risk. They've settled for something less. Don't wait. Don't settle for average. Don't let your giants wage war and win.

Pick up these five stones and engage. Move forward, make it happen. Do something that will change the course of your life. Do something that will outlast time and leave a legacy!

I will leave you with this thought:

Upon the plains of hesitation, beach the bones of countless millions, who on the threshold of victory, sat down to wait, and awaiting, they died.

About The Author

Curt is considered *"America's Master Sales Motivator"* due to his high energy, enthusiastic audience presence, and knowledge of sales motivation. He understands that motivation and knowledge can be combined to create the outcomes required to be successful. He communicates a balance that gives people the right tools to get and stay motivated.

Professionally, he has spent 20 years in sales. From building teams from the ground up, to Vice President of Sales of Houston's top computer integrator, he has been around the block. He has created successful teams, marketing programs, and exceeded sales goals as a professional

He is also a professor at the University of Houston, were he teaches Advanced Professional Selling. The Excellence In Selling program is the #1 program in the U.S for undergraduate sales development. Many universities and colleges are beginning to offer a structured track on selling and are using the ideas and courses from the U of H program as a model

Personally, he is a Certified Professional Behavioral Analyst (CPBA) with Target Training International. His study of sales and human behavior provides a strong foundation for his Leadership, Motivation, and Sales presentations. He is the author of *201 Sales Motivators*, a collection of quotes and short editorials designed to inspire and motivate sales professionals. Many of his written articles have appeared in newspapers and corporate newsletters such as Harvard Business Review Newsletter, Selling Power, Sales & Marketing Magazine, Sellebrations, Digital Dealer, and Houston Business Journal.

Audiences across America come away with new ideas, new tools, and a new level of energy after hearing Curt speak. His messages on Leadership, Motivation,

Customer Satisfaction, and Sales are offered in keynote, workshop, and seminar packages. When looking for real world experience and real world ideas, Curt delivers!

Giving The 5 Stones Back To Others

One of the best ways to help others see the value of 5 Stones For Slaying Giants is to share with others how you are using the 5 Stones in your business, career, and life.

We have created a special web site just for that. www.slaying-giants.com is the where you can purchase additional copies of this book and contribute back by writing a comment just how 5 Stones For Slaying Giants has helped you in these areas.

Go to www.slaying-giants.com and complete the form where we can have your comments and direct application of these stones. This would be a great benefit for others who would like to slay the giants in their lives.